# SUGAR BUSH BABIES

# SUGAR BUSH BABIES

## STORIES OF MY OJIBWE GRANDMOTHER

Janis A. Fairbanks

UNIVERSITY OF MINNESOTA PRESS

MINNEAPOLIS

LONDON

Published by the University of Minnesota Press
111 Third Avenue South, Suite 290
Minneapolis, MN 55401-2520
http://www.upress.umn.edu

ISBN 978-1-5179-1902-3 (hc)
ISBN 978-1-5179-1962-7 (pb)

A Cataloging-in-Publication record for this book is available from the Library of Congress.

Printed in the United States of America on acid-free paper

The University of Minnesota is an equal-opportunity educator and employer.

34 33 32 31 30 29 28 27 26 25          10 9 8 7 6 5 4 3 2 1

*In memory*

Nay-ta-baa-ca-co-na-mo-quay
Cecelia Robinson

# CONTENTS

# Prologue

ONE DAY, AT AGE THIRTY-FIVE, I sat on the porch of my home in Detroit, Michigan, listening to the rush-hour traffic passing by on the freeway, which was about six blocks away. Overhead, the sound of an airplane flying low as it approached Detroit City Airport growled its warning to the neighborhood that its landing was imminent. Cars pulling into nearby driveways put the dogs in the neighborhood on high alert as they began a steady crescendo of welcome to their returning masters. My tough little Pomeranian boss dog barked a command of silence to his younger packmates, a Doberman pinscher and an American pit bull terrier, who both looked at their foreman and flopped lazily at my feet, heads resting easily on their crossed, outstretched forepaws.

Although I loved the comfort of my pets, it suddenly struck me what a noise-polluted area a big city can be. I suddenly felt the need for tea and a biscuit covered with strawberry jam preserves. As I rose to go inside, I brushed against the cedar bush planted by the front door and instantly thought of my grandmother. The contrast between what I was experiencing now taking in the sounds of the city, compared to my time spent with my grandmother on her quiet homestead on the allotment property she had inherited from her mother and grandfather, came rushing over me. I missed my grandmother and the peaceful quiet of that country setting. The homestead was located on the shores of Big Lake on the Fond du Lac Reservation, and after I left Minnesota, whenever the stress of city living overtook me, I usually was able to restore my inner balance by closing my eyes and picturing myself standing on the shores of Big Lake, just a city-block distance from my grandmother's house.

Being by the water was bred into me, having spent my formative years on the shore of another Minnesota lake, Lake Winnibigoshish on the Leech Lake Indian Reservation in Bena, Minnesota, in a section of town referred to as "old Indian village." Our log cabin home was located within one city block of the shores of Lake Winnibigoshish, and the walk to it was rural. I remember seeing purple iris and wild-

My grandma, Cecelia Robinson, liked to have a clear view to the Big Lake shoreline from her front door on the Fond du Lac Reservation allotment land. She hired helpers to clear the brush. This photograph was taken in the 1970s.

flowers. There was also staghorn sumac. Wandering among flowers in the summer months was just the most normal, joyful pastime I recall, and taking that excursion in times of stress was all the medicine I needed.

Leaving the lush beauty of Bena and moving to Duluth, Minnesota, in 1951, when I was five years old presented a shocking discovery for me when I found out we were not just going for a ride: we were moving there where the yard had gravel and the streets contained a stream of vehicles passing by right outside our front door. There were no purple iris and wildflowers growing anywhere in sight, but one block away a house had a big green lawn covered with dandelions each spring. I could, and did, walk that block and make myself at home sitting on a stranger's lawn gazing at the yellow orbs of sunshine so profusely present.

Traveling from Bena to Duluth that day we moved did not disturb me, as I thought we were only going for a ride, as we sometimes did. We visited my mother's brothers and their families, who lived near Bena, and my dad's brother and sister and their families, who lived within a half-hour drive from Bena. What disturbed me was not coming home to Bena. We were in fact moving to Duluth. I saw runaway trees in the distance as I looked out the window of the moving car on the way to Duluth. In those days, cars had no seat belts, so I stood in the back seat, wondering why the trees were running. The effect of seeing evergreens in the distance while the car was moving made it seem like the trees were moving, and my five-year-old mind decided that they were not only moving but running.

Until that time, I had only experienced being around Ojibwe people in my immediate family in Bena, and I recall the total culture shock of being moved from a cloistered reservation to Duluth and its large population of white people, whom I had not encountered or interacted with before on a routine basis, although I had a white uncle who had white hair and piercing blue eyes that frightened me. I shied away from him when I saw him, which was frequent since he was married to my dad's sister. My Auntie Alma and Uncle Cliff lived in Bena, too, but they lived in the town part with their daughter, Molly, my cousin who had black hair and brown eyes like me, though she was half-white.

That year I ran away from kindergarten so many times that my mother had to go meet with the principal to explain my frequent escapes. "Where are you going?" they wanted to know. "Home. I'm going home," I replied. My mother said, "You are home," to which I protested, "This is not home. There's no lake, no flowers, no garden here." Only then did they understand I was talking about Bena, and the compromise was offered that if I agreed to go to school in Duluth, then any time school was not in session I could go to my grandmother's home on Fond du Lac Reservation. I readily agreed, so the plan went into effect, resulting in the creation of the warmest memories and most meaningful lessons of my life with my grandmother.

Accordingly, then, the final section of this book is set in Fond du Lac Reservation in northern Minnesota, when I was living with my grandmother on hereditary allotment property in a tar paper shack within a city-block walking distance to Big Lake. We had no electricity or running water, but we had sumac, wildflowers, and a garden. Grandma continued to work and maintain her vegetable and flower garden into her old age. I never felt poor living there, and Grandma read to me each night and told me stories that often contained lessons, which I learned to decipher for

Grandma stands outside the home her husband built for her, 1970.
She preferred to live here even after a new house was built for her by the
Fond du Lac Band in 1972.

myself. She rarely told me what to do and instead modeled
the desired behavior.

Grandma liked to speak Indian to me as often as she
could. She was a product of the government Indian boarding schools, and although the intent was to stop Indigenous
people from speaking their Native language, this did not
work with her. She was such a fluent speaker that everyone
on the reservation knew her or had learned language from
her. Grandmother gave me a greater exposure to Ojibwe
language and powwow dancing than I got in Duluth. She
spoke Ojibwe and was always teaching me new Ojibwe
words, and I could sit and listen when she routinely spoke
Ojibwe with her friends and relatives when they visited us.
I did not recognize it at the time, but after being away from
Minnesota I met city Indians who wanted to learn Ojibwe

and were interested in learning cultural practices. I began to set up language tables and social gatherings where Indians could mix and mingle while doing language and cultural activities, including drumming and dancing.

Potluck dinners were very popular activities, and those gatherings reminded me of the company Grandma and I had at the lake, where sharing a meal was always a component of our visiting. Something about sharing a meal and conversation says, "I love you. You are important to me. I enjoy spending time with you." This was a time of cementing identity among the Indigenous people. I took this lesson with me when I invested my time in community work at urban Indian centers as executive director responsible for planning services for Indigenous people in urban areas. Going to school and earning bachelor's, master's, and doctoral degrees supplemented knowledge that helped me serve my people, much like my grandmother had always served her community.

Grandma was a productive teacher, an activist champion for Ojibwe rights, and a driving force in Fond du Lac tribal government. She was the first woman to serve on the Reservation Business Committee. She was the grand matriarch for our extended family: she cared about what happened to all her children and grandchildren, and her influence was felt by everyone. Most important for me, she took ample time to always be there when I needed someone. She was and is my anchoring force to knowing who I am and in encouraging me to use whatever skills and talents the creator gave me for the good of our future generations. This is what has kept me grounded during my many life transitions.

My mom also was a role model, a determined survivor of adversity and injustice, and a pillar of strength. She instilled in her children the importance of an education and good grades. She did not comment on straight As: she expected us to get good grades, and I think we all just did it.

DURING MY EARLY LIFE, from 1946 through high school, there had been a noticeable lack of Ojibwe history books written by Ojibwe women authors. As I encountered historical accounts written by men and non-Indigenous authors, this lack of personal narrative oral history from the feminine viewpoint left me feeling a gap of warmth and love. Early school experiences made me determined to write my own history to counteract the often harsh, historical experience that I uncovered as I made my way through life. I decided to help fill this gap by authoring factual stories of my experiences for future Indigenous generations.

Did it occur to you that your life is living history? As I listened to the sounds of life in the big city on that day when I was thirty-five, I thought of the distinct phases I had already lived. I even wrote a poem about my impression, wondering what else was in store for me as I passed each new decade of my life.

As you move through your busy lives, I thank you for taking the time to read my stories. In this book I have written my stories as an Ojibwe girl growing to adulthood. This was during a historical era called Relocation, a time of transition from reservation living to urban living, a transition from being among only Ojibwe people to coming to terms with living in a multiethnic, urban area. The 1950s were influenced by Hollywood characterizations that created hatred, fear, and disdain of Ojibwe people that the child born in 1946 had to navigate to become an adult.

*Manoo bina.* That's okay. Hollywood movies of those years still exist, but so do I.

These stories contain the seeds planted in me during those early years that helped me blossom into an adult. Bena, Duluth, Fond du Lac Reservation: this is the path I

At age four, I stand in the family pansy garden in Bena, Minnesota, holding a fishing pole and minnow bucket. My mother liked to fish but I did not. I preferred to look at fish swimming and my mom relaxing instead.

traveled through girlhood. I would not be who I am today without having gone through the experiences I had growing up. Family experiences taught me that healing starts at home and that I should pass life lessons along to future generations as a part of an endless cycle. My parents, my siblings, and my grandmother gave me early childhood experiences that molded me, bent me in the direction I would lean, and I am enormously grateful to them. Mom and Grandma were busy women. They were also two women who took the time to model life lessons when the opportunity arose.

Grandma sits inside the tar paper shack, dressed in regalia, about 1973. My brother Ralph took this photograph, and he was an artist, so I imagine he set up the scene to be culturally meaningful. The television and my brother's brass bed tell me he was staying in the house by this time. The bare walls tell me that Grandma's pictures had been moved; she kept a picture of the infant Dionne quintuplets hanging on the wall. The light bulb wrapped around the rafter would have been wired to the electricity in Grandma's new house.

This book focuses on my grandmother, who joined the spirit world in 1986 but remains an inspiration to me in all I do. Learning from Grandmother gave me a lifelong set of values that has lasted even after she passed away. Those lessons and life experiences after I left Minnesota made me see that the lessons did not belong just to me. They were meant to be shared with other little girls I encountered, who deserved the kind treatment and loving lessons as much as I did. My mother loved me enough to release me to my grandmother to receive those lessons. My grandmother loved me enough to make sure I learned from her what I would need to survive in life. There is a certain strength in women that forges bonds and is the connection from one generation to the next, no matter how life circumstances may change. In the heart of busyness, making the time to pass along a lesson is imperative to the survival of the humanity not only of Indigenous people but of all people, who share the bond of humanity.

# *Bena*

BENA, MINNESOTA, is located on the Leech Lake Indian Reservation in northern Minnesota in the heart of the Chippewa National Forest. My life in Bena with Mom, Dad, my sisters, and brothers was from December 1946 to the summer of 1952, when we moved to the city when I was five years old. In a family of seven children, I was daughter number four, born just before my brothers started to come into this world. After me came a brother, and after him came twin boys. We were born each about two years apart, except for the twin boys, who were born fifteen minutes apart. They are two years younger than their older brother.

The government had encouraged relocation from the reservations to the cities for Indians, and my parents decided to make the move. It was not a favorable move for me. I was a country girl with no outside contact or influences there on the reservation. I was accustomed to seeing our log house, the dirt road leading to it, the cows and the cow pasture next door, the swampy area that held the beautiful purple irises, big Lake Winnibigoshish behind us, and the old lady who lived down the road in the next house.

We also had visits from family on Dad's side: Grandpa, Auntie Alma (Dad's sister) and Uncle Cliff (her husband), Uncle James (Dad's brother) and Aunt Ethel and their children; and family from Mom's side: Grandma, Uncle Earl (Mom's brother) and his wife, Auntie Lucy, and their kids, and Uncle Ray (Mom's brother) and his wife, Virginia, and their children. It was a cloistered little life for me, surrounded by a big family and beautiful countryside. It was very peaceful with the changing of the seasons and no responsibilities yet, just watching the days go by and getting to know those significant beings around the house who felt as comfortable to me as the earth, sky, and sunshine. We always had a dog, too. Our dogs had names like Blackie, Bozo, and Spotty. Mom always liked animals, and she was exceptionally good to them.

Mom had a domestic routine for cooking, cleaning, gardening, and taking care of seven kids that was impressive for a young woman who must have been only twenty-eight years old when we finally moved from Bena to Duluth. By the time we left Bena, Grandma, Mom's mother, had come into my life. She proved to be a splendid and lifelong influence on me. Mom didn't get the benefit of Grandma's influence as a girl, as her dad had taken her and her

The Fairbanks children in 1950, along the side of our log cabin home in Bena. Left to right, standing: Patricia, Phyllis, Ralph, Janis, Arleen. In front: identical twins Gerald and Gary.

brothers to live in another town with his second wife and their family. And besides that, Mom had attended one of the Indian boarding schools for a year, before Grandma intervened and said Mom should go home. So there was yet another influence in Mom's life that may have cut into her emotions. Indian boarding schools were well known for their lack of compassion and coldness toward the Indian children who attended them.

So many of the questions I had as a youngster as to how two women so closely related could be so different were answered late in life for me—when I understood that Mom didn't always have Grandma there to mother her. When Mom married so young, at only fifteen, her responsibilities multiplied so fast: she had to exert a lot of effort in the direction of getting training and a job to help support the family financially, which took its toll on the emotional support she might have been able to offer us then, if she had had the time. I never felt particularly close to my mother until late in life, toward the end of her life, when she finally let down her guard and allowed me to get close to her, as I had always longed to do.

As for Dad, he was fifteen years older than Mom, and we were his second family. He was a widower quite young and always mourned the loss of his first wife. But he was good to us kids and told me wonderful stories about his and Mom's marriage when they were first married. One story I remember was about him and Mom before any of us were born. They lived together and had a little dog, so after work he would routinely stop at the store and buy three pints of ice cream: one for him, one for Mom, and one for their little dog. He loved her and never remarried again after she and he were divorced after twenty-three years of marriage.

My mom, Alvina
Fairbanks, holds
me, sometime in
1946 or 1947.

Daddy's little girl:
my dad, William
John Fairbanks,
holds me around
1948 in Bena. Our
dog Spotty was
always nearby.

City life was not for him, and I believe the effects of living in the city caused him great unhappiness. He lasted eight years in the city, then returned to the reservation. He had a quiet life after the divorce, returning to Bena to make his home and living with his sister until he died in 1975, just a month before his sister did. They are buried in the same cemetery just across the road from each other. Dad rests under a tall evergreen tree close to the location where our family lived in 1952, where memories of that family life still seem so fresh even after all these years.

BENA WAS KNOWN as a good location for fishing, and tourist cottages were just a block or so away from the shores of Lake Winnibigoshish. In Minnesota, the Land of 10,000 Lakes, it isn't far to go fishing anywhere, but for us fishing was in our backyard. Lake Winnibigoshish is the fifth largest lake in Minnesota. Fishing is really good in a lake that size. The people who rented the cottages during the summer paid to go fishing, while we, because we were Indian and lived on a reservation, lived there year-round and ate fish from that lake, too, because Mom liked to fish.

She told me she tried to teach me to fish once, but she couldn't get me to fish. I remember going with her to sit under the railroad overpass by a river. I was about three, four years old. That fishing spot wasn't far from our little log cabin home. We walked there. Mom didn't drive in those days. She didn't drive for a long time, even after we moved to the city. She was wearing a very colorful skirt and sitting on the bank of the river with a stick in her hand. I thought my mother was beautiful. She had soft black hair, and she put pin curls in it to create soft waves. Being in the sun all summer made her

skin glow with a nice coppery softness, and when she smiled
it was like seeing a rainbow after the storm. I liked sitting
next to her as she sat on the bank of the river holding her
fishing rod: she looked so happy and peaceful. Fishing must
have relaxed her from her daily routine of caring for her husband and seven kids at such a young age.

The stick was, of course, her fishing rod. It had a line
hanging from it and the line was dipped in the water. Every
once in a while, she would pull on it a little, then sit some
more, watching the water, while I watched her and admired
the way the wind played with her hair. After a while, I ran
through the grass looking for beetles and butterflies. There
were dragonflies in the field, too, and I loved to see their
transparent rainbow wings when they landed long enough
for me to look at them.

Imagine that! Mom trying to teach me to fish, when all I
did was run around making noise and scaring the fish away.
Instead of getting the idea that the stick with the string dan-
gling in the water was to catch us food, what I wanted to
do was look at my beautiful mother, the river, the sky, the
grass, the bugs, and, yes, even the fish as they swam near the
shore. No wonder I remember her taking me with her just
that one time. My twin brothers, four years younger than I
was and babies in Bena at the time, both loved to fish. They
were better students than I of the fine art of fishing when
Mom took them later, when they were older. As adults, they
all still loved to fish and used a boat so they could go where
they wanted to fish. I got to eat of their fish, and I like fish,
but I feel like I'm killing them when I take them out of the
water. I am definitely not a fisher person.

Mom walked everywhere in Bena. I remember walking
with her to the general store in town next to the post office.

We had to go past a fence with huge German shepherds behind it. Those dogs were so big and barked so loud—I was always afraid to walk past that part of the road. But Mom picked me up and carried me. The dogs got loose one time, but all they did was bark at my feet that dangled just below Mom's waist as she shouted at the dogs to go home. Gosh, Mom did care and guard me, even though she had all of those other kids, too.

I HAVE MEMORIES of my older sisters from when we lived in Bena. Most are very mundane, like walking down the dirt road to the water with them, watching them swim, having my oldest sister take me to the schoolyard to play, or watching the three of them pick berries. All of us used to go to the end of the road to wait for Grandpa's car, and then ride standing up on the running board the length of the driveway to the house. It was a risky business, even though Grandpa went slowly when we jumped aboard. One time I fell under the car and gripped the running board extremely hard until the car came to a stop. Grandpa couldn't hear the other girls hollering for him to stop, and I could see the rear tire of the car about a foot away from my shoulder, so I kept a firm grip, knowing that if I let go that would be the end of me. The Indian hospital was about twenty minutes away in Cass Lake, so off we went to get an X-ray of my arm. I remember looking up at the bright light in the hospital and my arm hurt when they positioned it for the X-ray. I blamed the light for making my arm hurt. But that cured me of riding on the running board again.

A couple of memories are painful and scary, like riding on the running board. Another vivid and scary memory is the time I ran away from my dad when I saw that the garden was on fire. Where I had been used to seeing vegetables and green leafy things growing one day I saw instead a path of fire and smoke making its way across the garden. I had been on my way to the outhouse when I saw the fire, and I walked toward it for a minute, until I got a whiff of the smoke, then I turned and ran as fast as I could toward the outhouse, which was not too far from the edge of the garden. I heard footsteps heavier than my own running faster in my direction. I looked back and saw my dad gaining on me. I tried to run faster, but just as I got to the door of the outhouse my dad caught up with me. He swooped me up in his arms and carried me away from the fire, back toward the house. As it turned out, the fire was a planned burn to get the garden ready for the new growing season.

My older sisters Arleen (left) and Patricia Fairbanks outside Bena Elementary School. This picture was taken around 1950, before our family moved to Duluth.

Dad and Mom always had a garden. They planted vegetables for us to eat and pansies for us to look at. We always had bumblebees buzzing around the front door because we had flowers growing there. I don't recall bees ever stinging me or my siblings. I'm surprised that I didn't get stung, because I always liked to look at insects closely. But they knew that I was no threat at all to them. So they left me alone.

We spent a lot of time outside. Dad was a carpenter, and Grandpa was a carpenter and boat maker. On the reservation, people needed boats to harvest wild rice, so Dad kept busy building, repairing, or painting boats. Any time I smell sawdust, lumber, or paint, I think of my dad. He was one of the happiest carpenters I have ever known. When he worked, he sang. He had an impressive bass voice, rich and full of timbre, and he knew so many songs. He would be painting a boat, always using deep green paint, and singing "Red Sails in the Sunset."

He liked to take little breaks and stop to eat a lemon or peel a cucumber. He had very precise methods for doing either one. For the lemon, he would sit down and roll the lemon along between his hand and his upper thigh. Then he would cut it in half and sprinkle salt on it and eat it. For the cucumber, he would cut off the ends, rub them against the part he had cut them from, and then throw the ends away before he peeled it and ate it. I liked the way he could make his jaw snap when he took a bite. It seemed such a manly thing to do. Daddy was someone you could talk to. He had a deep sense of humor, and he liked to play with words. When he said he wanted "Yung-yung," we knew he wanted onion. He could say the words right—he just liked to say something else.

His sister, Auntie Alma, was just as full of fun as he was. She lived in Bena, too, so we got to visit her. She lived in town on the main street in a white house with blue shutters, and she had lots of flowers in her yard. There was more of a town in those days. We had a train depot, a schoolhouse, a drive-in theater, a general store, a post office, and a beer joint, as they were called back then. We also had two gas stations: a Shell and a Standard station. My oldest sister and I share remarkably similar memories of free ice cream cones from a man named Leo at one of the gas stations. We agree that the ice cream cones came from the same place, a red, white, and blue Standard station, and that the flavor was vanilla. But the man named Leo that she remembers wore a hat with a slick bill on the front, drove a Greyhound bus, and stopped at the station for gasoline.

The man I remember named Leo wore a hat with a slick bill on the front, worked at the Standard station, and pumped gasoline for people. My sister is six years older than I am, and I was age five and younger when I walked to the gas station, so my memories might not be as accurate as hers. But if my Leo drove a bus, he sure didn't go on the road often, because every time Dad stopped at the station for gas, Leo would come out and pump it for him. Daddy would go inside to pay for the gas, and I would go with him. Leo would smile down at me, and pretty soon he would head for the wafer cones and silver scoop that he used to dig ice cream. I suppose there were times when Daddy paid for my cone, but there were also times I would go into the store by myself, and Leo would dip me up a free cone.

My oldest sister says her Leo, the bus driver, gave her a free ice cream cone every time she was there when the bus stopped at the Standard station. "He must have felt sorry

The historic red, white, and blue gas station in Bena, Minnesota, where we went for gas and ice cream cones. In the early 1950s, this paved road was dirt; Highway 2, which passes in front of the gas station, was paved.

for the poor little Indian girl," she told me. I wondered if my Leo gave me free ice cream cones for that reason. I suppose we were poor little Indian girls, but somehow those words made us seem so pitiful. I didn't feel pitiful, growing up in the country and walking around in fields of flowers. And anyway, Dad worked at the Standard station, in a way. He was a carpenter who also painted all the cabins that the Standard station people owned and rented out to tourists in the summertime. My godmother lived in the main house by the cabins, so she may have been the owner or related to the owner of the gas station. I think that's why I got free cones; I don't know for sure. I had a good and thoughtful godmother, for even after we moved to Duluth, for years she used to send me birthday cards with an embroidered handkerchief tucked inside.

I always liked visiting old ladies. They usually were calm, quiet, and said or did interesting things. There was one old lady who lived at the curve in the road by our driveway. I liked the inside of her house. She had lace everywhere, along with a tick-tock clock and a wooden rocking chair that sat on a big, braided rag rug, as they were called. When I visited her, sometimes I got to watch her eat. She would sit in that rocking chair and work on her bread to make it edible. She took the crust off, flattened a portion of the white bread with her fingers, and put the flattened bread on her tongue, like a Catholic communion wafer. She didn't chew it, so I guessed she must have just let it grow soft and juicy from her saliva before she swallowed it. Her house was quiet except for the slight creaking of the rocking chair and the hollow-sounding tick-tock-tick-tock-tick-tock of her windup clock. I didn't like the feeling of the room unless she was in it. The movement of her fingers as she flattened the bread was somehow comforting.

My brothers were there in Bena, I know, but I don't really remember any particular interaction with them at the time. From the pictures I saw later, they were cute little guys and a big hit with my oldest sisters, who are pictured carrying the boys around when they were babies.

Grandpa, too, must have liked having all of us around. He was patient with kids and played card games and checkers with us. He liked to chew snuff, and it was fun to watch him aim for his spittoon and make the brown snuff juice stream right on track for its target.

Yes, I loved the environment in Bena, nestled away in the country watching creatures going about the uncomplicated business of living. There was the feeling of a life cycle in the regularity of the change of seasons, the snowfall that

Celebrating my brother Ralph's first birthday in Bena. I'm at left and my sister Patricia is behind Ralph.

shut everything down for a while and left beautiful swirls of ice crystals on the windows, only to gradually give way to longer days and spring blossoms. I could count on the grass growing tall and green and seeing the birds getting ready to build their nests again. In the summer, I could count on seeing Mom and Dad busy with gardening and outdoor chores.

Everything felt in harmony, peaceful and predictable. I was not in any way prepared for the momentous changes that were coming. Luckily for me, a year or so before we moved to the city, Mom's mother, my grandma, came for a visit. How well I remember becoming aware of meeting her. It was on a summer day when Dad took a couple of us kids with him to the train station to pick her up.

I WAS ABOUT FOUR YEARS OLD the year I became aware of Grandma. She had seen me when I was a baby, or younger than four, but this visit was different. Grandma took very decisive actions that made me know that I was a special person to her. That type of support came at just the right time, for I was about to go through an enormous change during the next year, and having Gram in my corner gave me a decided edge in overcoming unexpected challenges.

The earliest recollection I have of seeing Grandma was at the train depot in Bena, where we picked her up from her journey from her home in Sawyer on the Fond du Lac Reservation. She came down the steps carrying a shopping bag with what I later came to recognize and refer to as "the brown goodie sack" peeping out between the grips. I watched curiously as the well-groomed, slightly stout lady with the navy-blue straw hat made her way toward us. My dad told me to say hello to my grandmother. My grandmother, instead of nodding and dismissing me, as I thought she might do, surprised me by leaning down to kiss my cheek. Her lips lingered for a moment. Then she reached into her sack and gave me a huge piece of fruit. That orange was the first gift of oranges I was to receive from her over the years, and it was all for me. I was not required to share it or save it for my baby brothers. Gram gave it to me. I was special. After that first visit from Grandma, I looked forward to our occasional trips to her home on Big Lake.

Being with Gram was a significant difference from feeling like sandwich filling, being the middle child, with three older sisters and three younger brothers. It was a strange position to occupy, being the baby sister to the girls yet being the little mother to the boys. With Grandma, I was just me. All of my life, she cared for me deeply, and she let me know it. Meeting her in Bena, just before Mom and Dad moved us to the city, came at a suitable time for me. Grandma was my key to get back to the country life I loved so well. Because of her, I regained my little paradise and expanded the whole concept by being around her, listening to her stories, and learning from her.

Postcard photograph, date unknown, of my grandma wearing regalia. My grandmother loved to dance and she took me into the dance circle when I was a very young girl. Many happy hours were spent dancing at powwows.

Someone once said to me, "You can take the girl out of the country, but you can't take the country out of the girl." I hope they meant it as a compliment, because in my case it's true. The tranquility and beauty of a country setting were etched into my consciousness during my formative years. The lessons from nature were later reinforced by lessons from Grandma.

All I have to do to go back to the reservation is close my eyes. I can still see the country roads, the log cabin house, the gardens, and the way we lived back in 1952. The old Standard station is still operating, and the red, white, and blue cottages are still standing. In 1979, those structures were designated as a historical site, so I hope they will be preserved. The road to Lake Winnibigoshish is still there, although the road leading to the old homestead is no longer visible. Trees now stand where that road and the old log cabin once stood. But the last time I was there, I stopped at the Standard station in Bena for a vanilla ice cream cone.

Seeing these places and experiencing the memories they bring never lose their charm.

## DADDY WAS A LUMBERJACK

ONE OF MY EARLIEST MEMORIES is of my dad wearing a plaid shirt, chopping wood. He was always working with wood. He had a big two-handled saw that he used to cut logs in pieces. Who was at the other end of the saw was not important to me. I just looked at my dad, elbows bent with both hands gripping the big saw handle, pushing and pulling until a piece of the log fell to the ground. I might have been a bit of a nuisance, hanging around so close to the work area, but he never chased me away. I had to be all of three or four years old at the time. Daddy looked so tall to me, I thought he could do anything.

Only one time do I recall being afraid that he would get hurt. He was getting ready to load wood into a trailer, and to do that he had to move the trailer over to hook it up to the car. He picked up the trailer by the front beam and lifted the beam straight up in the air. It was taller than he was when he did that, and I thought for sure it would fall on him. I thought he was in danger, so I started crying. He looked at me and lay the trailer beam back down on the ground as fast as he could, loped over to me in two or three bounds, and scooped me up in his arms.

"What's the matter?" he wanted to know.

"I'm scared, Daddy. That thing will fall on you!" I cried.

"No, no, don't be scared. I won't let it fall on me!" He brushed away my tears and pushed my bangs out of my face. They fell right back again, but it felt good to have him brushing his hand across my forehead. He sat on his chopping block stump and held me until I stopped crying. Then he told me I could watch if I stayed sitting on the stump until he was done hooking up the trailer. I said okay, and he went back to work.

He chopped wood, too, for our woodstove at home, and he built ricing boats, so he always smelled like sawdust and fresh paint. The boats he painted were green, dark green. He whistled and sang while he worked and took breaks to have a cucumber or glass of lemonade. When he made lemonade, he took a lemon and rolled it against his thigh four or five times before he cut into it.

In the days before I was born, Daddy was a lumberjack. I have one picture of him pulling a toboggan through the

The Bena homestead, 1951: the garden gate, the family car, the trailer Dad used to haul lumber, and the Fairbanks children, plus one cousin. In the back row, Patricia holds Jerry and Arleen holds Joe; I'm in the front row at left, with cousin Rose Robinson and Phyllis. The back of brother Ralph's head is in front.

snow. The toboggan was loaded with logs, and Dad was facing the load, walking backward, pulling. He was so strong, and all of that physical activity must have kept him in decent shape, because he was not fat. He wore a hat that had a crease in front and a bill tucked under the crease. I thought he looked just dandy.

By trade, he was a carpenter. Sometimes, after we moved to the city, I got to go on jobs with him. I saw him climbing through houses that had no walls or floors, only outlines of where the walls and floors would be. He always made sure I had a safe place to sit, then he went to work, measuring, marking, sawing, hammering, whistling, and singing. He was one of the happiest workers I ever saw. His voice was deep and had its own echo, and he knew at least a hundred songs. He kept a three-ring notebook filled with

pages of handwritten lyrics to old songs. His script was precise and ornate, like he had practiced for hours to get the
letters to look uniform and legible. Daddy had gone to one
of the Indian boarding schools when he was a boy, so I imagine he did drills on everything to try to get it just the way
the boarding school people wanted it to be. He didn't talk
about the boarding school experience very much, just told
me the name of the place, and that's about it. He attended
Flandreau Indian School.

He told me one time that he didn't like the way they
taught history. Every time the Indians won it was a "mas-
sacre," and every time the whites won it was a "victory." He
didn't like that, but you couldn't argue with the teachers.
They were always right, no matter what.

Daddy had a pretty hard life, I think, having to be an
Indian man during a time when society viewed Indian men
as enemies of the people. I'm not sure that time is completely gone or will ever be completely gone. As long as
there is a collective guilt over land theft and so forth, there
will be a tendency to blame the oppressed people: it's easier
than taking responsibility.

After we moved to the city, Daddy was not as happy
for extended periods of time, and although he still sang his
songs and whistled while he worked, there often was a far-
away look in his eyes. It was better when my cousin's cousin
Darrel worked on projects with Dad for a while. They both
laughed often, and they dug up the whole area under our
kitchen, which was destined to be an extension of the basement. While they dug, Darrel liked to throw worms at me,
then laugh while I ran away. I always came back for more.
I liked to watch Darrel eat toast. He had the whitest teeth,
all straight and strong looking, and he would crunch down

evenly when he took a bite. It just made me want to eat toast, too.

One day, Darrel went away. He was only seventeen when he joined the army and a short while later was shipped out to Vietnam, where he was killed in action. He died there when he was only twenty-two years old. Such a young warrior.

Eventually, Dad moved back to the country and lived with his sister. He seemed more at peace in the country and spent time teaching young apprentices the carpentry trade. I visited him once or twice and saw that he had gone back to being busy with wood and painting—not boats but houses, as he remodeled interiors of homes and painted the finished rooms. His sister's house was a fine example of the color choices that were not the run-of-the-mill neutrals but bold colors that coordinated well with each other and had a feeling of life to them. He painted turquoise walls, mango walls, leprechaun green walls—rooms that were fun to enter.

They're all gone on now, Daddy, Darrel, Auntie. Even the house is no longer there. Ah, but the memories, the songs, the colors, the smell of sawdust and paint, and the picture of the young lumberjack. Those are all still here and remind me of the happy times of my daddy, the lumberjack.

## SUGAR BUSH BABY

GRANDMA LIKED TO TELL ME the story of where and how she was born in 1895. The location was out in the woods at Deadfish Lake, about four miles from the homestead allotment property. Her mother and a group of women were working at Deadfish Lake on the Fond du Lac Reservation. They were busy with sugar bush, where they were gathering maple sap to make into maple syrup and maple candy, when Gram decided to make her appearance in this world on March 11, 1895. The weather was typical for northern Minnesota, late winter, with cold nights but warm days, just right for the maple trees to give up their sap.

Sugar bush was centered on wherever the pit was dug for making a fire and boiling the sap that had been gathered from the sugar maple trees. Ojibwe people had to gather ten gallons of sap and boil it for four hours just to make it yield two pints of maple syrup. Trees had to be tapped and buckets had to be hung from them to let the sap accumulate until the buckets could be gathered and taken to the boiling pit. My great-grandmother was in the middle of all this business when her labor pains started. The rest of the women helped her prepare for the birth of her baby, my grandmother.

Gram explained in great detail how a new pit had to be prepared with a couple of support poles buried five feet apart with a strong stick laid across the support poles for great-grandmother to hold on to as she crouched in an upright position to give birth. The pit was lined with fresh cedar, and my great-grandmother had to hold on to the strong stick to await the birth. There were no trips to the hospital in those days for the Indian women. They just stopped long enough to give birth, then cleaned themselves and their babies and went back to making maple syrup. Gram liked to make sugar, and I expect this process always reminded her of her mother as she went through the same business of getting enough cans and taps to gather sap each spring. My sister has an old newspaper clipping of Gram at sugar camp standing over the big pot of boiling liquid that would yield syrup and candy, depending on how long she boiled it.

Grandma was one happy, proud, and productive Chippewa woman. Besides bearing eight children, including my mother, an aunt who died as an infant, an uncle who died as a boy, and five other uncles who followed various paths outside the Indian world, inside the Indian world, or walking a precarious path in both worlds, Grandma took an interest in her grandchildren and great-grandchildren as they arrived.

The Robinson family, my grandparents, mother, and uncles, around 1927. Standing, left to right, are Raymond, Grandpa Fred, and Donald. Seated, left to right, are Earl, Grandma Cecelia holding my mom, Alvina, and Donald.

She wanted us to take an interest in each other, too. After I left the reservation at age nineteen and moved to another state, I didn't see my cousins very often. Grandma would send letters or messages informing me of what the cousins were doing or would have one of the cousins call me to tell me current news. She once sent me a letter a cousin who had moved to California had sent to her, telling me that the news would let me know what Eileen was doing. Eileen was about my age but had married at age twelve and had a large family of her own. Grandma said it was important to keep up with what was going on with our relatives. I always thought so, too, and took a keen interest in their tragedies and triumphs, always trying to find out where they were and what they were doing with their lives. The threads of kinship spread in all directions and resulted in an interesting and thriving bunch of talented people. We had nurses, teachers, linguists, retail people, craftspeople, artists, musicians, carpenters, armed services people, civil servants, domestic specialists, and even a writer or two in our far-flung family. Grandma was always proud of everyone's accomplishments. She made the ideal grand matriarch. Her way was to give to anyone who needed something, often going without so that someone else wouldn't have to.

She carried this trait over into hospitality for visitors, too. I remember one old Indian lady who came to visit us, right around suppertime. Gram had fixed a fish for our supper, and we were about to sit down to eat. The old lady came walking up the road, looking hot and tired, so right away Grandma poured her a cup of tea and asked her to come in and sit down. The lady sat and sipped her tea, looking at the platter of fish as she sipped. Gram got down another plate and silverware for our visitor and served a portion of fish for her. The old lady ate the portion, then Gram asked her if she wanted another piece. She did, so Gram served another piece: then another, and another, and finally the last piece. We sat sipping our tea, waiting for the old lady to finish eating. She looked rested and happy when she was done eating. Gram offered her more tea, and they visited while I cleared the table. The visit lasted an hour or so. Meanwhile, Gram and I hadn't eaten. We had no more fish. But it was more important to see to the needs of a tired, hungry old lady than to worry about our own stomachs at that time. I knew that without Gram telling me, just by watching to see what she did when our guest arrived. After the lady left, fortified for her walk home, Gram made us oatmeal for supper, and we really were unaffected by having waited a while to eat.

## Powerful Beings Live in the Sky

THE ROLLING OF THUNDER always reminds me of my grandmother. The story she told about powerful beings that live in the sky was a fantastic way to explain the sounds that usually came before a heavy rain, and thunder that could be accompanied by lightning.

When the clouds rolled in, we went into our little shack and closed the curtains. Gram lit the kerosene lamp, and we settled in to listen to the thunder and the raindrops echoing off the rooftop. With the house as small as it was, the roof was just two to three feet above our heads. The raindrops pounding on the roof sounded as close to us as a modern-day shower when you're standing in it. I like the sound of rain. It always makes me feel cozy. The thought of fresh water being collected in the rain barrel at the corner of the house filled me with anticipation of laundry day, when the water would be used to wash our linens and clothing. That was always a pleasant, leisurely day of activity and visiting for me and Gram.

As the raindrops fell and the thunder rolled, Gram told me a story. "Listen. The giants are bowling today," she said. I looked at her and waited for the rest of the story. "The giants are bowling today?" I prompted. She was heating water for tea, and she moved the pan of water over so she could add another split log to the fire. She had a wadded-up towel around the pan handle as a heat shield, and she carefully moved the water back to the hot spot on the stovetop. "On a day like today, when you see clouds gathering, it's from the dust the giant's shoes make when they go to their bowling spot. The lightning comes because giants walk with a harder step than others, and it makes a spark when their heels touch down too hard. They get excited on bowling day."

"Then what causes the water that makes the raindrops?" I wanted to know. "Well, Jaa'iins," she started tentatively, as she got the teacups ready. "The water is formed from the sweat the giants work up from walking to their bowling spot. But the giants know how to make the sweat turn into pure, clean rain because they know we need clean water down here to wash with, to drink, and to swim in. They also know that we need good clean water to make things grow."

"Good," I said. "I don't want to be drinking giant's sweat—or washing with it either."

"You're not, my girl." She smiled and poured the hot water into our teacups. We had freshly baked biscuits to eat with our tea and strawberry jam to put on the bread. The rain was falling steadily and the rhythm on the rooftop had a soothing quality. The rumbling had passed over us and was fading in the distance.

"Why does the bowling spot move? I can tell it's moving because the sound is getting farther and farther away."

"Do you think we're the only ones who need water?" Gram asked me. "The giants are very wise and know how to move their magic to where it's needed."

"Oh," I responded, looking at my bread to admire the shine of the strawberry jam before I took a bite.

Gram always knew how to entertain me when the weather stuck us inside. We were outdoor people routinely, but when rain came we had a routine for that, too. As the raindrops became a whisper on the rooftop, we drank our tea and enjoyed the warmth of the fire. The quiet whispers soon faded, and I was left to ponder the mystery of how the giants could turn sweat into pure water—another wonderful gift of nature.

One of the most wonderful qualities I found in Gram's stories was her ability to take a concept and put it into a framework that I could understand. While we never went bowling ourselves, we knew what a bowling alley was and how bowling balls sounded when they thundered down the alley toward the pins. Even the sound of the ball crashing into the pins gave a credible imitation of a lightning strike outdoors. So her story enabled me to picture a game in the sky that I could relate to, while she fashioned a tale that helped me to understand the importance of rainfall to the survival of people and the planet. She was truly an expert storyteller. And she was very adaptable to the changing surroundings and circumstances of life. Those qualities and others made her a very cherished figure in my life, both then and now.

## THE GREAT FIREBALL

STORMY WEATHER meant two things to me. Giants were bowling again in a great mystical game to bring us pure water. And, it was time to draw all of the curtains closed and cover up the mirrors. The Great Fireball might wander through the house, and if the image were reflected in a mirror there was no telling what might happen. Nothing good could come of it. So when storms were coming, we went in the house, closed all of the curtains, threw a towel or blanket over the mirror, and made sure we had dry wood in the house to keep the woodstove going. As we had no television or radio or stereo or electricity, our entertainment was talking to each other or reading. We talked. Reading was pretty well reserved for close to bedtime. And sometimes, storms came early.

Conversation is a great device. Words are fun and can be played with. Images can be created and evoked from the simple fabric of a string of words. And, oh, how Gram and I loved to string our words together during a storm! She told me that we were pretty safe from fireballs and that they were known to form up around Inger and Bena. I knew that must be true because Dad had told me the same thing. "Watch out for fireballs," he said. "Traditional people think fireballs are formed when someone is mad at you, and if you see one coming, get out of the way. You don't know who that might be."

Someone told me that medicine people know more about fireballs, and I'll bet they do, but even if I knew any more about them, I wouldn't care to say any more about them. It's enough to know that they exist, and in a storm close to your house, draw the curtains, and cover up the mirrors. That

way, you'll never have to see a fireball in your house and
wonder, "Who goes there?" Stay out of harm's way.

## BOAT RIDE ON BIG LAKE

EVERY SO OFTEN during the summer, Gram and I would
go for a boat ride. We would go in a big wooden boat, with
a couple of paddles, that was tied to the dock. My dad built
the dock, and the boat, too, as it was a flat-bottom model,
the kind they used for ricing. There was no wild rice in Big
Lake, so this boat must have been a pleasure boat for Gram.
It was painted green, but it was old so there was only faded
green paint left on it. Still, it didn't leak, so when we went
for a ride, I felt safe.

Gram had me get in the boat first and go to the far end
to sit, then she got in, looked to make sure the paddles were
in place, sat down, and untied the boat.

She took her time paddling across the lake, making the
ride slow and easy. It was so pretty. There were cottages on
the other side of the lake, but that side of the lake was not
densely populated. A road went around the lake, but not
close enough to see from the water, so our view was mostly
trees and natural shoreline. In the water, lily pads floated in
patches, with white and yellow spiked flowers growing on
the deep green foliage. I always looked for frogs on the pads
but seldom saw any. There were schools of sunfish close to
shore, and little schools of minnows swam close together
and all in the same direction. If one turned, they all turned.
I wondered how they knew it was time to turn and how they
let each other know that it was time to turn. It was like they
were attached to one another by invisible string: give it a

tug and all would turn and go in another direction at the same time.

I liked to lean over and trail my fingers in the water, but Gram didn't want me to do that, so I only did it once. She was afraid my leaning would tip us over. We didn't wear life jackets, and I didn't know at the time if she could swim. I could dog-paddle and stay afloat, but I wouldn't want to experiment with how long I could do it. I never saw Gram swim or even wade in the water. We were leading a dangerous life to go paddling across the lake without life jackets if neither of us could swim. But here I am. I've lived to tell the tale.

We used to go visit a fellow named John who lived across the lake and gave haircuts. Gram never got a haircut, but I did. She told John to keep my hair all one length, falling about to the shoulders, with a full set of bangs. I was young when we went for those haircuts. I recall a warm day when Gram told me to go for a swim to wash the short hairs off before we went back home. I hadn't brought a swimsuit and I said so. "Just go in your bloomers," she said. "You're just a little girl, and nobody can see you here." I didn't want to go in just my bloomers, and she could see me here, I thought. But Gram was Gram, and she was my boss. So I stripped down to my bloomers (I liked her word; I thought it sounded better than "underpants"), and I ran into the water and sat down with my back to the shore. When I finished washing the short hairs off, I crawled toward the shore. Gram was looking at me.

"If you're done, stand up." I looked toward John's house to make sure no one was outside. I was cold now and I had goosebumps on my arms. But I had on nothing but bloomers. I didn't want anyone to see me in my bloomers. Gram saw me looking around. She said, "Oh, Janis! You're only eight years old! You ain't got nothing to hide!" Maybe not, but I was almost naked, and when I stood up my bloomers were wet. You could almost see through them. Jeez! I ran to Gram and grabbed the towel, wrapping it around me. I made the towel into a tent, then took off my wet underwear and put on my dry clothes as fast as I could. I stayed away from the house until it was time for our boat ride home.

The ride home was just as peaceful as the ride there. Watching the dragonflies come to explore the boat, the paddles, Gram's hair, and my knee was fun. I tried to be still so the one that landed on my knee would stay a while: I wanted to see his colors up close. But there was nothing to eat on my knee, and soon he flew off, hopping across the water, lifting up the bugs that made themselves so obvious by making little trails at the surface of the lake, leaving little wakes as they swam. There was so much going on that I had to find just one thing at a time to concentrate on or I would see nothing at all.

I wanted to draw pictures of the things I had seen, but nothing I put on paper compared to the beauty of the real thing. The colors looked drab, and the water didn't ripple and shimmy the way it did in real life. No, the best thing to do was just look and remember, I decided. So I locked those memories inside my brain, along with the emotions they stirred, for later, when I needed a comfortable place to go.

# Duluth

IN DULUTH, MINNESOTA, at age five and a half years old, when we entered the house on First Street where we would live for three years, I marveled at the indoor toilet that had a chain hanging from the high-up toilet tank: when you pulled the chain, the toilet flushed. We had not had electricity or running water in our log house, but in this new house there was both. Still, I didn't like it. The small yard was all gravel and there was a wooden porch right up to the doorway. Back home in Bena, we could step in from outside where there was no gravel or wooden boards to walk on. It was plain, soft mother earth.

I never questioned why people called where we lived the "Bowery." I just went along with the description and referred to the places I went on First Street and Superior Street in Duluth as "walking around in the Bowery." After research, I now know it is a reference to its similarity to "the Bowery, a street and area in New York City, historically noted for its cheap hotels and saloons and peopled by the destitute and homeless." That is from *Webster's Unabridged Dictionary* in 1996, and it is a pretty accurate description of Duluth's bowery in 1952.

We were a poor family when we first came to Duluth, so we lived in the low-rent district in a two-family house. Behind us was an apartment building where our landlady lived, and behind that was an alley with crumpled remnants of other brick buildings. Broken bricks and broken glass were playthings to us, and colored glass counted as treasure to one of my brothers and me. We collected it.

We lived across the street from the fire station, and a couple of buildings away from the station stood an old hotel. We had a wooden boardwalk across the street from us, and wooden steps that led down the hill to Superior Street, where the local beer joints were. In the middle of our block was Joe's gas station, where I used to go with my pennies to get peanuts from a machine. At the end of the block, Mork's grocery store was a handy place to get popsicles in the summer.

Duluth was a big city even in 1952. There was so much to see that I had never seen before, and noise from traffic, because the house my parents rented was less than a block away from one of the main thoroughfares in the city, Mesaba Avenue. But luckily for us, across the big avenue and up the hill around the corner was a vast expanse of boulders, grass, shrubs, and trees for us fresh-from-the-country kids. We all went to "the rocks" (as we called it) to sit and watch cars, trucks, trains, buses, and ships pass by. Duluth had all of that. It was quite a difference from watching grass sway, trees budding, bumblebees hovering near the front door, and cows chewing their cud in the pasture of the house next door.

Duluth, Minnesota, was built on a hill, and people refer to it as the San Francisco of the North, to give you an idea of what the terrain is like. There are steep hills, and grain trucks would often lose their brakes as they made their way down the avenues to the loading docks in the harbor or on their way through town. In the winter the streets were icy, and vehicles had to use chains on their tires to navigate the hills. It wasn't unusual to see parked cars wearing blankets on the hoods and outdoor light hook-ups plugged in, leading to the engines to keep them from freezing.

I didn't like all the cars passing by right in front of our house all the time. It was just so noisy. We lived only one block from the Duluth Civic Center, so the street was always busy. During the gateway renewal project of the 1950s, the city demolished our rented house along with all the buildings on both sides of the street between Fifth and Sixth Avenues West. A new traffic light was installed on the spot where our front yard at 621 West First Street was located prior to construction of the second lane of Mesaba Avenue. According to an article on the urban renewal project, the city planners of Duluth wanted to demolish several buildings in our area to break up the section of town known as the Bowery, which contained twelve establishments with liquor licenses. After the renewal, they granted the twelve licenses again, but the businesses were interspersed throughout the city to prevent the development of a new Bowery. When I was young, ages six to ten years old, I wandered around in the Bowery and didn't feel any threat from the citizens who liked to go to the beer joints. I went there to sell lilacs, and some of the guys would buy them from me. Some would give me a big grin and laugh as they handed over their nickels, as if they knew me. I was drawn to the people I recognized as Indians and felt less lonely in the city.

MOM AND DAD HAD SEVEN CHILDREN, and I fell in line as the fourth daughter, followed by three brothers. My three older sisters had all started school by the time we left Bena,

and my three younger brothers had enough time to accli-
mate to the city before they started school. I was the only
one plucked from the country and immediately plunged into
a strange school with strange-looking beings called classmates who said and did strange things. I experienced what
I now know was complete culture shock. I had lots of quick
learning to do. My parents had both attended the Indian
boarding schools. They both talked little of their boarding
school experiences, but they came away with a determina-
tion to take care of their children and not to send any of the
children to that kind of school. Ours was the first generation
in our family who did not go to boarding schools. Instead,
we went to public schools in mainstream society.

The school I went to when we first moved to Duluth was
on Second Street, about five blocks from where we lived. We
didn't have school buses, so we walked to and from school
through all kinds of weather. Crossing guards were on duty
to help us across the streets during the school year, but on
weekends and during the summer we were on our own.

It was an awful risk crossing the street by ourselves
because we were so small, barely big enough to be visible
over the hoods of cars, so we always tried to cross where
there were streetlights. My sister Pat walked us to the store
we went to most often. It was located across the street on
the corner at the opposite end of the block from where
Mork's stood. It was smaller, but we shopped there more
often when we wanted to get something. Pat is four years
older than I am, and she was always taking care of us littler
ones. She was good at it and always talked nicely to us.
Going to the store with her was an educational experience
because the little corner store had everything we needed to
buy for groceries.

Our family in 1956, photographed at the College of St. Scholastica in Duluth. Standing, left to right: Patricia, Phyllis, Arleen, Janis. Seated, left to right: Gerald, my mom Alvina, my father William (Bill), Gary, and Ralph. Photograph by Sister Noemi Weygant, O.S.B.

A tiny little old woman worked at the store, and she was always chewing something. I wondered if it was snuff, but Pat said no, and I never saw the old lady spit brown juice, like Gramps used to do when he chewed snuff. So she just liked to make chewing motions while she worked. She had a huge knife and hand-sliced the bologna we ordered, then took a big enough piece of brown paper off a roll that hung on the wall to wrap it with. She called me "The Jenna" and would ask where I was when I didn't go to the store with Pat. She liked me enough to give me a gumball once in a while. I really liked it when old ladies gave me a nickname. It made me feel special. I always liked listening to the old ladies talk, too, because they always had interesting stories to tell.

Another old lady who liked me was our landlady. She lived in the brick building behind us in a little apartment filled with things that were fun to look at. I went to visit her when Dad put in cabinets for her. She told me stories about when she was a little girl my age and showed me a doll she said she used to play with. I looked at her very closely, and it seemed I could see a little girl about my age peeking at me through those watery eyes. How could that be? But I felt a little girl there again when she ran her finger over the cheek of the little doll. It was only about two inches tall and made of porcelain. It had a pale white skin color and wore a white lace dress. The hair was also porcelain, a pale-yellow color that had short sculpted waves. The facial features were round, as were the eyes, but the mouth had very tiny bow-shaped lips. I looked at the doll each time I visited her, and I told her stories about my life in the country. She said I looked like a happy little girl, and we sat and had cookies and milk while we talked.

Later, before we moved away, I went to tell her so long. I didn't like to say goodbye. I still don't. It sounds too final. So I went to tell her so long. She put her hand on my shoulder and stood by me for a minute. Then she went to her little cabinet and got the doll she had shown me. She handed it to me and said, "Take good care of it." She wasn't Indian, but she sure was nice, just as nice as Gram, I thought. Do people have to be old to be nice? Does it take such a long time to learn how to be nice to other people? Would my hair have to be white before I could talk to little kids and make them feel good? No. I decided the time to start was now. I know what it feels like to be treated bad and I know what it feels like to be treated good. Good is better.

I found out that there are good people in the world,

and they aren't all Indian. They don't all hate Indians, and sometimes hurting us can be an accident.

My sister Pat wasn't always there when we wanted to go to the store, so sometimes we would just go by ourselves. One time, my brother decided to cross the street by himself. He got hit by a car. He must have been only five years old, and he was smaller than I was, two years younger. He was on a mission. He was on his way to try to return a bird's nest to a tree that the neighborhood kids had taken it from. The nest had eggs in it, and I remember looking at the tiny eggs before my brother said he wanted to take them back to the tree. Off he went, and the next thing you know there was a big traffic jam in front of our house, backed up from the corner where my brother had tried to cross. The nest with the little eggs was shattered by the impact of the car hitting him, and we were all so scared that he wouldn't come home from the hospital. I remember praying and making bargains with God to just let him come home and I would take loving care of him.

He recovered. The man who hit him felt so bad! Mom said the man called on us often to see how Ralph was doing. It was nice to know that the man really cared about my brother.

In Bena, my dad was my strength. He called me Daddy's little girl, I suppose because I was the youngest girl, but it made me feel incredibly special when I heard him say that. He whistled and sang while he worked, and as a carpenter and boat maker his work was often in our front yard. In the city, his carpentry work took him away from the house, and I felt lonely without him. Mom was busy going to school and studying, so sometimes we children depended on each other for care and companionship until Mom graduated from nursing school. My older sisters one by one married and moved out to start their own families, while I cared for my younger brothers until they too moved away to another state in their early teens.

I did enjoy playing with all three of my little brothers, and I knew if anything happened to any of them we would all sorely miss them. One of the games we used to play was Band. I got the idea from watching a big parade that had a couple of marching bands. The bands looked so fine in their school uniforms, and I liked the way their feet kept exact time with the tunes they were playing. I thought I should teach my brothers how to play something, so they agreed to play band. Dad got us little plastic instruments, and I made sounds for the boys to try to show them how their

Nursing school graduation, Miller Memorial Hospital, Class of 1953. My beautiful mother is in the second row, third from left, wearing the all-white uniform of the day with a freshly starched hat, white stockings, and white shoes. These were professional women, ready to save the world.

instruments would sound if they really played. Ralph was my best little band member, most obedient and smart when I told him how to hold his little plastic saxophone during our rehearsals. The little boys, the twins, tried to manage their instruments nicely, too, but they were only three years old and fumbled around with the little guitars they were supposed to be playing.

I used to sit them on the front step by the sidewalk and pretend I was the conductor. I used a Popsicle stick as my wand and directed them as they tooted on the sax and twanged on the little plastic strings of their instruments. Dad told me he had driven by one day while they were sitting there, and he had seen me conducting them. Years later, the twins and I really were in a band at the junior high school we attended. They both played the tuba, and it was quite a treat to see them wearing their band uniforms and marching down the street. Ralph was not in a band, but he later taught himself how to play the piano. I wonder if they remember the little practice sessions we had when we were so young. The three boys were all about the same size, so many people thought they were triplets. Dad called them the three bears. I liked looking at them because they were so cute. All three were very bright and caught on quickly to most anything I was teaching them.

I couldn't do advanced activities with the twins when they were three. They were too little to go anywhere, so my play routines involved Ralph. He liked to go up the alley with me to explore the brick ruins for treasures. We looked for bits of broken glass in assorted colors to collect as pirate's gems. He liked to tease me by finding spiders and pretending to eat them. Daddy longlegs were his favorite prey. I didn't mind looking at the spiders, but I begged him not to eat them. He would grab one gently enough so he wouldn't hurt it, then he cupped his hand over his mouth as though he had slipped the spider inside. He then proceeded to make chewing motions with his jaw, cheeks, and lips. I learned soon enough that he only did it to hear me plead for their lives, so I devised ways to torture him as well. It was a companionable pastime, playing tricks on each other, and I was sorry when peer pressure pulled my brother away from me: the day came when we no longer roamed around together because he was a boy and I was a girl. Pretty sad reason, I think. But it was fun while it lasted.

My older sisters and I rarely did things together. I was a drag on them, as I was too young to hang out with them. I recall one time my sister came with me to the library to get my library card. I had to sign it myself, so she stood beside me and whispered the letters I needed to print on the card to print my name. I really thought that was nice of her to do that for me. It was the only way I could check out my own books, and I went to the library often. I spent hours sitting in the children's section, looking at books even before I had learned to read. That was one thing I liked about the city. I had access to books. I was curious about whether my sisters remembered me as a kid, so I asked my oldest sister if she remembered me in the city. She said she remembered me going to school there. Yup, that's what I remember, too.

There were times we all did get together outside to play games in front of the house. There was a sidewalk there to draw a hopscotch grid on, and we did. We used pieces of broken brick to make the outline and found our flat rocks up in the alley. Another Indian family lived down the street from us, and those girls would come over to play hopscotch every so often. We also played something called

Draw a Magic Circle, a form of hide-and-seek. And the old stand-by, jump rope. Each game provided a little physical exercise, but not as much as the games we played when we were in the country.

We couldn't go home again to Bena, but we still had a country setting to pursue country-kid doings at Grandma's house on the nearby Fond du Lac Indian reservation. At Grandma's house, we could go swimming in the lake or take long walks in the woods. We would sometimes go to swim at the resort next door, as there was a longer dock and sandier bottom in the swimming area there than we had at Gram's landing. I didn't especially like to go to the resort because there were so many summer tourists there, and they weren't always friendly to us. I used to wonder why white people who didn't like Indians would even come to the reservation if it made them so miserable to see us. But I noticed that often what they did defied logic, so I didn't ponder the question too long. The tourists had cabins and could change into their swimsuits inside, while we had to bring our suits through the woods, then change in the resort's restroom and leave our clothing lying on the beach while we swam.

One time as we were leaving, the resort owner's daughter came running across the lawn waving a pair of bloomers, yelling, "You dropped this!" at the top of her lungs. Everyone on the beach looked up to see what I dropped. I grabbed the bloomers and tucked them inside my towel as quickly as I could, wishing that people would be a little more modest about such items as bloomers. They are not something that anyone should wave around in public. I thanked her for bringing them to me and then ran home as fast as I could.

When we were at Grandma's house, we often played Ante, Ante, Aye Over, a game that consisted of throwing a ball over the top of Grandma's little shack to the players on the other side. If the opposite players caught the ball, they had to run around the house and try to tag one of the players from the side that had thrown the ball. If the ball failed to go completely over the house, the player who missed the throw had to confess his or her error by hollering, "Pigtail!" when the ball rolled back down from the roof again. Then he or she could try to throw it across again. All of the throwing, catching, hollering, and running gave us ample exercise. Grandma was as tolerant as she could be of our game, and that was quite a feat of restraint on her part, because the ball bouncing across the roof while she was inside visiting with the parents of the players must have been pretty distracting. But we were in the country, and we aimed the ball high, and it was made of soft rubber, so there were no windows broken.

Sometimes during the summer Gram visited the family on First Street in Duluth. She babysat all of us while Mom was going to nursing school and Dad was working. She navigated the city well on foot, but she didn't like it as much as her home in the woods. She could be a tough adversary when someone crossed her, even though she stood only about five feet tall. When Mom and Dad worked, Gram stayed with us, cleaning and cooking and looking after us. She scrutinized the company we kept and let us know if she thought someone wasn't fit company. She especially didn't like "roughnecks," as she called people who were partial to cursing and acting uncouth. The neighborhood kids tried to be on their best behavior when she was around so she would allow them to play with us. Sometimes accidents would happen, though, and a kid would hear words somewhat similar to those that I grew up with.

There was the time a softball game got out of hand and the softball flew through our bathroom window, smashing the glass while Gram was in the bathroom. We could hear her exclamation clear in the living room, two rooms away. "Hooh!! Who done that??" We heard tinkles of glass hitting the floor as she brushed herself off and came walking out of the bathroom with the softball in her hand. She took inventory of our little brood. We were all standing there looking at her. She went back into the bathroom and looked out the window just as the neighbor boy came walking over, looking for his ball.

Looking at Grandma, and at the broken glass, he said, "Have you seen my ball?" She held his ball up in her clenched fist and replied, "How could I miss it? It came flying through this window here and almost knocked me out! I'm going to keep it until you come back here with your parents. You can't go around breaking people's windows without offering to pay for the damage! Go get your parents and don't come back here without them!" The boy mumbled, "Sorry," then turned to go.

Gram stuck the softball in her apron pocket and went to get a broom and dustpan. She came back, set the broom and dustpan down, and proceeded to brush shards of glass out of her hair. She turned to look at us, asking if we knew who the boy was. We told her the kid's name and waited around to see if he would come back. He did, bringing his dad with him. The two adults talked, and the man examined the broken window. He agreed to have it fixed. The boy apologized again before Gram gave him back his ball, admonishing him to be more careful with it. "Someone could get hurt. You should be playing at the ball field with this."

I TRIED TO LISTEN TO GRANDMA and other old ladies when they said anything, because I learned that they had information they willingly shared, and they usually made sense. This was not always the case with younger people. When I started meeting kids other than siblings and cousins and neighbors on the reservation, I learned that not all children had learned to be nice, and an unfortunate block of them liked to be mean in words and deeds. I learned to distract the meanness out of them with simple stories. They were more curious than mean after a while, so I counted on their curiosity to overcome their need to be mean. As time went by, I could see that much of the meanness was caused by an irrational dislike of Indians. I concluded that it was not the individual's fault and that with insight those individuals might understand that we are people, too. Not all good, not all bad, just people who eat, sleep, laugh, cry, just like anyone else. But I had learning of my own to do about people who were not Indians.

An early lesson was learning that people with blue eyes can see. That lesson really sticks out in my mind. People with blue eyes can see! I was only in first grade when it was pounded home to me in a way I will never forget: that blue eyes don't always mean blindness.

Before moving to the city, while living in Bena, our family always had a dog. My experience with our dog Blackie is tied to a valuable learning experience with my classmates in Duluth. Blackie lived a long time. My parents had him even before I was born, but in the end he began wandering around bumping into things. Blackie had long, wavy black hair and gorgeous deep brown eyes. But when he started bumping into things, I noticed that his eyes had turned blue. I asked Mom what was wrong with Blackie. Why had his eyes turned blue, and why was he always running into things? She said Blackie had gone blind—he couldn't see anymore. So we had a blue-eyed dog that couldn't see. With brown eyes he was able to see. Our family all had black hair and brown eyes. We could all see. I made the connection that blue eyes meant blindness.

Early on, at age six, I guess, I noticed a certain girl in my first-grade class had golden hair, the color of the tops of cornstalks growing in Grandma's garden, but oh, the poor girl had blue eyes. She dressed neatly and acted pretty calm, which I liked to see in a person, and one day I noticed she had on a pink dress just like the one I was wearing that day. The only difference was that she had a matching fabric belt and I had a brown etched leather belt. I wanted to tell her to look at the way we were dressed but knew that I couldn't because she couldn't look. She had blue eyes. She was blind. While I was puzzling over how to let her know that we were dressed the same, I was looking at her, staring at her, I guess, and thinking.

Suddenly, she made her eyes wide in my direction, jutted forward with her chin, and stuck out her tongue! Oh, gosh, she can see! Blue eyes, but not blind. I need to ask Mom about that one, I thought. She told me Blackie was blind. His brown eyes had turned blue. This girl has blue eyes, but I know now that she can see. What's going on? Bit by bit, piece by piece, the puzzling little robots took shape in my mind. I could see that they grew uncomfortable around someone they considered rude, just as I did. I could see all shades of gray, green, blue, light brown in their eyes, and feel better for them, knowing they could see.

When I started school in the city, I looked at the other kids in the class and thought how strange they looked. Their hair and eyes were all distinct colors. There were no other Indians in my class, so I was extremely interested in how these other people looked. I noticed the teacher controlled the class. The children sat quietly and responded on cue. "Good morning, children." "Good *morn*-ing, Miss Smith," they all replied in unison, droning out the syllables in a most unnatural cadence. I thought that particularly odd but went along with it. I was always busy trying to find commonalities with the other children, so I studied their actions and their mannerisms and the way they talked and dressed for clues. And it wasn't only the white children I studied, once I found out they existed. I started paying closer attention to what the Indian children back on the reservation did or said or looked like, too.

My third grade class from Jackson Elementary School in Duluth. I am in the second row, third seat from the back, wearing a black and white dress and glasses. By third grade, I had grown accustomed to my classmates and was able to connect each one with individual characteristics. Marilyn had a mom who always brought us cupcakes, Mary Jane sang soprano, Bobby's mom was a nurse, too, Donnie liked my stories, Ray had a twin, Jimmy's grandma ran the corner store, and so on. Remembering details was a skill Grandma taught me.

Grandma knew that I did this because I did it even when I was with her. Once when I was about ten, we were visiting somewhere, and I asked her why this one Indian family had two daughters who looked so much alike, except one had black hair and brown eyes and the other had blonde hair and blue eyes. You could tell they were sisters by their facial features and bone structure, but the difference in the hair and eye color mystified me. Were these girls really sisters? Was one of them adopted? How could one have blonde hair and blue eyes when both parents had black hair and brown eyes? Grandma said, "Well, there must have been 'hankie-pankie' there."

"Oh," was all I could think to say. "Hankie-pankie" had no meaning for me at the time, but it sounded like a good explanation to explain a mystery.

Another time, when I was about the same age, we were visiting an Indian family that had two daughters a year or two younger than I was. They lived in one of the cottages by the lake, and they looked like I expected Indian girls to look, but they acted too strange for me to want to go near them. They talked incessantly and jumped on furniture and ran around in the house. The one closest to my age came over to where I was sitting and bent down to peer into my eyes. I looked back at her but didn't say anything. She went over to Grandma and asked, "Can she talk?" Grandma told her I could. The girl wanted to know, "Well, if she can talk, why isn't she saying anything?" If the girl had said something to me, I would have answered her. But she didn't. She asked Grandma about me, as if I were not even there. I thought, "How odd." In my mind, I answered, "Yes, I can talk. I just don't want to talk to you." People who talk about people in the third person when that person is sitting in the same room and could be addressed directly are suspect for their lack of manners. Anyway, I want you to know that I wasn't thinking that only my new white classmates were strange. I was noticing variations in Indian children's looks and actions as well. I was looking for commonalities, too.

By the end of first grade, though, I knew I had to find a way to get them to let up on the "squaw" business. It was the 1950s and the television Westerns were no help in creating decent images of Indian people. I found out early that I was an exceptionally good reader. Grandma's bedtime stories were responsible for that, and for sure she taught me to love the written word. I could see different endings to the stories we read in class, so I began to experiment with changing story endings. Then I began to create my own stories. By the time I got to second grade, I was authoring stories on a regular basis. I was a storyteller.

At last, a great commonality! My classmates loved to hear stories, and I loved to tell them. My new nickname became "Ye old storyteller." I liked it!

## SELLING LILACS ON THE BOWERY

IT COSTS A NICKEL to get a candy bar. Where am I going to get a nickel? It's late springtime and the days are getting warmer, even though we have dense fog sometimes and the lilacs are not all fully open yet. They sure are pretty. I wish they bloomed all year long. I bet they are my favorite flowers forever.

Hey, I know! If I like lilacs so much, they will make a nice bouquet for somebody. I can sell flowers and get a nickel for a Milky Way. I know where I can get lilacs. There are lilac bushes everywhere around here, even up on the rocks. I'm old enough to cross the street by myself, as long as the light is green. Off I go to get the lilacs.

I've got the lilacs. Now I have to go down to the beer joints and wait outside to find a buyer. Here comes an old Indian guy. He looks like my dad, only shorter and heavier, that's how I know he's Indian. He smiles at me and his brown face crinkles as he says, "Anishinaabe." *Anishinaabe* means something like "Indian," only in Chippewa. I knew I was Indian, but how did he know? I wondered. "Do you want to buy lilacs? Only a nickel," I offer. He is still smiling as he digs in his pocket and takes out a nickel. As he hands it to me, I try to hand over the lilacs. He waves them away with his hand and says, "Gaawiin, you keep them." I start to hand the nickel back, but he says, "No, you keep the nickel, too." I thought, "Good, I can sell them again for a nickel and get enough for two candy bars."

How did that guy know I was Indian? And why would he buy my flowers, then let me keep them anyway? Big people are so hard to understand sometimes. I'll know more later when I get that big. Right now, I'm six years old and I just earned enough to buy my own candy bar.

## LIFE ON EIGHTH STREET

AFTER FOUR YEARS IN THE BOWERY, we relocated to the East Hillside neighborhood where my parents purchased a house. We had only one car and the move allowed Mom a short four-block walking distance to St. Mary's Hospital where she worked. Dad had to use the car to get to his different assignments to do carpentry work. For me and my siblings, we eventually had to walk a mile each way to go to school. Washington Junior High and Central High School were across the street from each other, so the walk was the same for four years for each of us who attended those two schools. That was rain or shine, as there was no money for bus fare. The walking didn't seem so far; it was just cold during the winter. But what carried me through these changes were usually words from my grandmother. For the weather, she would say, "Bundle up!" For other kinds of challenges, she would say, "God helps those who help themselves." She was not one to cast out pity when adverse situations arose. She expected all of us to rise to the occasion and work it out.

I remember being in the new house with Mom, cleaning it up before we moved in. We were sitting on the floor in the room I would share with my sister, taking a break from washing the floors and woodwork, and Mom had spread a towel on the floor to hold our lunch. We had a fine lunch of canned Spam, sliced tomatoes, white bread, and milk. For dessert, we had apples. Mom had finished nursing school by the time we moved and was truly knowledgeable about nutrition, so we had well-balanced meals in reasonable proportions. None of us was fat as children. We had ample exercise, sharing household chores and playing outside when we were young.

After lunch, we continued to clean rooms and get ready for move-in day. Compared to Gram's little palace in the country, the tar paper shack, I thought Mom and Dad's house in Duluth was a big house. It had three bedrooms upstairs and one bedroom downstairs. Mom designated the upstairs bedroom areas: the front bedroom was for the older girls; the small, skinny bedroom was for the younger girls;

Mom in her flower garden on Eighth Street, circa 1962. Wherever she went, Mom always planted flowers. The house in the picture was across the street from ours. These are sweet memories.

This picture was taken in 1959 when I was twelve years old, riding a bike I borrowed from my sister. We lived on a corner lot with lilac bushes, a mountain ash tree, rose bushes, and raspberries that Mom planted. Across the avenue are other houses in our neighborhood.

and the room at the top of the stairs, a nice fairly square shape, was for the three boys. The downstairs bedroom was for Mom and Daddy. We had a middle room, as we called it, which held the couch, television, and stereo, along with a big round wooden table with wooden chairs. The room was big enough to hold an upright piano, which Daddy had accepted in exchange for his labor on one of his carpentry jobs. There was also a large kitchen big enough to hold a table for nine people, as we all ate our supper together with Mom and Daddy when we were kids. The kitchen had a walk-in pantry, which made it handy for grocery storage and big pots and pans. There was also a basement where Dad hooked up the washing machine. The basement had an entryway from under the porch, as many of the homes on the hillside did. Dad later put in an addition to the basement, as he liked to keep busy and was skilled at carpentry and building.

As I said, Daddy bartered his labor in exchange for other things in those days. I recall one day he brought home boxes of beautiful costume jewelry for Mom that he had accepted as payment for another job he did. He liked giving things to Mom. His favorite gifts were items that his pretty young wife liked to wear. Besides the fancy jewelry, he gave her a couple of jewelry boxes. One was made of wood and the other was covered with black ultra-shiny laminate and had lift-up shelves in it with various size compartments for necklaces, earrings, rings, and pins. I loved looking at that sparkly jewelry as much as I loved looking at the agates I collected when I was in Big Lake with Gram, or the broken bits of colored glass I had collected as a young child. Sparkles remind me of the stars at night or the glistening of snow after a fresh snowfall. If I close my eyes, sometimes I can see the sparkles of the natural beauty nature gives us in such abundance. To that beauty, of course, there is no real comparison, but still, I have a great affection for looking at colored glass and rhinestones.

I had a great affection for looking at my mother, too. Once in a while, Dad and Mom got together with the neighbors across the street to go out somewhere special. Mom would wear her jewelry and the White Shoulders perfume that Daddy had given her. I used to close my eyes and think of Mom actually having white shoulders, and it always made me giggle. Mom had such nice skin, and I liked the color of her skin. I would describe it as a natural medium-to-dark tan, which looked particularly good on her. She looked even darker when she put on her nurse's uniform, which was all white in those days, including nylons and a starched nurse's hat. She was a very efficient nurse and worked in the emergency room at St. Mary's Hospital in Duluth.

She wore glasses, too, which I always thought made her look very smart. Sometimes, she pushed herself too hard and got overtired. I recall seeing her stretched out sleeping on the couch, too tired to even go to bed after work. I got in the habit of taking her glasses out of her hand as she slept and laying them on the table by her head. I didn't want to disturb her, so I got a blanket and covered her as she slept. My poor, tired little mother—I watched her sleep and noticed that her nose was shaped just like Gram's nose.

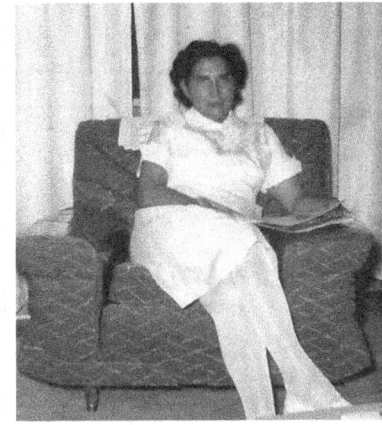

Mom was a hard worker and was proud of her nursing profession. Here she is in a rare relaxing moment before she leaves for work, in 1963.

It was hard being away from Gram during the school year, and it was hard being away from Mom and Dad during the times I was not in the city attending school. I knew that in the old days, before Indians had to be "tamed and civilized," that families had all lived and traveled together. I couldn't really see an improvement in having the family so fragmented and separated from each other. Everyone was busy with different things, learning different things and focusing on different values. How could that be an improvement?

The best times to me were the times we were all together for wild rice harvest. Nobody had to miss anybody. And everyone shared in the work and the feast afterward. It was the same with deer hunting. We were all together, with the men doing the hunting, the women doing the cooking, and all of us doing the eating . . . together.

We got the togetherness in Duluth, but Gram was missing. She didn't come to stay in Duluth when I was going to school, except once in a while. I missed our talks and her stories when she wasn't there. Still, there was togetherness in Duluth at suppertime with Mom, Dad, sisters, and brothers. Mom saw to that. Mom was an incredibly good cook and made it a point to serve supper each night at about the same time, and we all sat at the table together. Daddy sat at the head of the table, with Mom to his right. We ate and talked, then took turns doing dishes right afterward, so we had a good routine going to get everything done and in order. I always remembered Gram's little saying, "Many hands make light work," when I was doing the dishes with a sibling.

By the time I was twelve years old, it had become my job to make lunch for myself and my three little brothers.

Grandma visits our home on Eighth Street in Duluth, 1962. She always dressed so neatly and usually wore an apron, but here she takes time to read and relax.

We lived only half a block from Franklin Elementary School, so we walked home each day for lunch. I usually fixed peanut butter and jelly or bologna sandwiches and we had white milk. In those days, about 1958, people weren't so concerned about whole milk versus 1 percent, 2 percent, or skim milk. Once in a while we had soup and crackers and chocolate milk for a change.

Mom and Daddy had set up a charge account at the corner store a block away from the house, so if we wanted to we could go to the store to buy groceries and put it on the bill. Sometimes I decided to buy little individual pies or cupcakes for my brothers and me. The storekeeper used to tease me when I went in and charged up four or five pies. "Is that all you do? Sit around and eat pies all day?" "This isn't all for me, Bee. It's for my brothers and my dad, too."

I liked to get an extra pie to put in Daddy's lunchbox. They weren't expensive, only ten cents each, although if I wanted to be really thrifty, I could buy cupcakes, or "snowballs" as we called them, and share them, for they came two to a package. But Daddy didn't mind if I bought the pies, and I know he liked them for lunch because he told me so. He may have spoiled me a bit, I don't know, but I liked it when he called me Daddy's little girl.

I really enjoyed being with him, watching him work, hearing him sing, or hearing him talk. In the evenings, we would sometimes watch boxing on television. He talked about the boxer's moves and told me about the days when he was a Golden Gloves boxer in school. He must have really enjoyed his boxing days, as he talked about them often. He talked about school days once in a while, telling me that one teacher had called him "Will-yam! Will-yam Fairbanks!" He could do great imitations of voices and mannerisms. He could imitate his dad's voice and mannerisms extremely well, to the point that even when Gramps wasn't there, my dad could make him seem to be there by talking and acting like him. It was great fun.

Dad and Mom usually worked different shifts, so one of them was home with the kids. They took on separate roles with us, with Mom becoming the disciplinarian and Dad becoming the quiet, fun-loving nurturer for us. He liked to tell stories and make jokes. He referred to our dog as a "mangy cur," but he was good to her. When the mangy cur had puppies, he was very gentle with the pups. When the female dog was in heat, Mom confined her to the basement to prevent puppies, but determined male dogs can find a way to meet their mates.

The entryway under the front porch came in handy when something or someone wanted to sneak in or out as inconspicuously as possible. That entryway became a steppingstone to one of our prettiest female dogs. She had a litter of puppies that came about from a neighborhood cocker spaniel's ability to find a way into the basement from under the front porch. From a short-haired gray terrier female and a long-haired black cocker spaniel came a gorgeous gray, wavy-haired female pup that we kept and

Me at age fifteen in our house on Eighth Street in Duluth.

named Tootsie. Dogs were welcome in the household, and later in life, Mom liked cats as well, but in the early days we had no cats, except Felix.

One night, Dad got locked out of the house accidentally, and no one knew he was outside until he came walking up the basement stairs with a big grin on his face when he knew he startled us. "How did you get in the basement?" we wanted to know. "I was locked outside, but I'm like Felix the Cat," he replied, still grinning. "I can get in anywhere!" Daddy was like that. Minor inconveniences didn't upset him. He just found a way to work around them and kept a sense of humor about it.

As time went on, the older sisters started to leave the household, and each time I went away and came back to Duluth, I could see that changes were taking place. Soon a major change would occur that would cause the household to dissolve and disappear forever.

Divorce changes everything. And divorce changes nothing. I still loved my parents, still mourned the loss of a cultural way of life that could have kept things intact, and still held fast to the things my grandmother had taught me over the years. Without those teachings, I may have felt that there was nothing to hold on to. But life goes on and there is a plan for every life. There is a job to do.

## Girl Scout Camp

When I went to school in Duluth, one of my classmates convinced me to join a Girl Scout troop. I was in the fifth grade. That summer the troop went to camp near a local dairy, and we stayed there for about a week. The Girl Scout leaders planned different activities, and I found the whole experience interesting but not particularly enlightening.

One of the activities was to walk in the woods and collect leaves, then mount them on paper and try to identify the trees the leaves came from. I dutifully gathered the leaves, carried them back to camp, mounted them, and printed the name of the tree each came from. I finished the project quickly, talking to the leaves in my mind, thanking them for the shade they provided and the beauty of sight and sound they had given us while they were on the trees. I studied the veins in each leaf and the tiny bite marks on individual leaves and thanked them again for bringing life and food to the insects that had dined on them. Then, having finished the project, I looked for something else to do.

There was a stack of slender reeds in our communal area, so I gathered a handful to play with. As I examined the reeds, it occurred to me that I could make something from them, so I began weaving them together. One of the Scout leaders came to look at what I was doing and told me that the group would be learning to weave from the reeds when the leaf-labeling project was done. Learning to weave? What's weaving? I wondered.

When the other girls had finished their projects, the group leader called them over to where I was working. She picked up my basket and announced, "Now, here's a girl who knows her weaving!" The girls looked at my "toy" and asked me where I had learned to weave. So, this is weaving! I told them that gathering grass and making things with it was something I had always done. I didn't know I could earn a badge by doing something I had always done. I also decided that I needed to learn more words and made a pact with myself to read the whole dictionary. I never completed that project, but I got a surprisingly good start by browsing through it once in a while. It was more fun to play games like Scrabble and complete crossword puzzles, and through that process I learned more words and meanings quickly.

One of the other outings we had while at camp involved a tour of the dairy farm. We saw the cows, the milking machines, and the huge dairy cans where the milk was collected. I liked seeing the cows in the pasture. It reminded me of the old pasture in Bena where the neighbor's cows grazed. I didn't like the sight of the cold-looking milking machines attached to the cows' udders. And I didn't like the sight of the small stalls where the cows were contained in the barn. I wanted to see them outside grazing in the pasture or lying in the shade of the trees, resting, and taking life easy.

I did enjoy the camp experience, especially walking in the woods. Being around so many city girls was a valuable experience for me. It made me understand how lucky I was to be able to go for walks in the woods as often as I did at Gram's. I didn't have to wait for camp week to look at leaves or gather grasses to make things.

At the end of the camp, I decided to drop out of scouting. I wanted more time to spend out in the country at Gram's. Camp was good for girls who needed to learn how to identify leaves and weave. I already knew how to do both, and I learned it from the way of life I shared with Gram.

## HONOR ROLL DAYS

GRAM SAID IT WAS ALWAYS IMPORTANT to learn new things and do my best at it. Time was not something to be wasted or squandered. So I did my homework, studied my lessons, read voraciously, continued to author stories that didn't all start with "Once upon a time . . ." and tried to do a little extra work in school so I would learn all that I could about a subject. The result was a good report card. I felt especially proud of my efforts when the first marking period of sixth grade came.

Our teacher announced that he had never given a student straight As on the first marking period, but one student in the class had done all of the work, done well on the tests, and earned all As. So he had given that student all As. The other students were looking around the room to see who the culprit was, while I sat quietly waiting for the card to be handed to me. I knew it had to be me because I knew I had done all of the work and had scored As on my tests. I hoped that the card wouldn't earn me any enemies. This was my third and last year at a new school and I wanted to keep a low profile if I could. I hadn't been called any unkind names for years now, and I didn't want it to start again. Oh, one kid called me Slats because I was slender, but it didn't seem unkind. Slender felt good.

When the teacher announced my name and the card came my way as I had expected, none of the kids seemed incredibly surprised. And the results were good, because on any team assignment, more students wanted to be teamed up with me! What a pleasant surprise for me.

That honor roll status lasted through the whole sixth grade. I well remember that one sixth grade teacher who recognized and rewarded my arduous work.

## GOING TO THE CIRCUS

SHERRY WAS A REDHEAD, Karen was a blonde, and I was a brunette. Sherry had a pale aqua blue windbreaker, Karen had a red one, and I wore a black sweater. I wanted a white windbreaker but settled for my usual long-sleeved black sweater. I imagined it went with everything, so I wore it often. We were getting ready to go to the Shrine Circus, and I felt very glamorous, being one of three long-haired beauties, just like the ladies who wore sequined costumes and stretched themselves so elegantly just before they flew across the center ring on their trapezes into the waiting arms of their well-muscled male companions.

Well, we were only eleven and twelve years old, so we had to take the bus. Sherry was the eleven-year-old, and Karen and I were twelve. Sherry was a grade behind us in school. We formed a friendship that lasted five years, until we were about sixteen, when I got a boyfriend and Sherry moved away. So many changes we went through in so few years, though.

Anyway, Sherry was really the beauty of the three of us. She had that auburn hair that shined and shimmered in the sunlight, like brand-new copper pennies in a pool of clear water, and her eyes were wide and green with little flecks of brown. She lived in an apartment complex with her mother, a parakeet, and a cat. The complex was on Second Street, just one block from the civic center and the police department and the county jail. It was a fun place to hang out because we could go to the civic center and walk in the halls of the buildings and listen to the click-click-click of the ladies' high heels as they walked down the halls. Or we could go outside and walk on the ledges of the concrete walls that lined the steps of the inclines around city hall. Or we could crawl up on the huge statue that sat in front of the court. Ah, the simple pleasures that we enjoyed back then.

Sherry was, for an unknown reason, extremely interested in being sexy. She was only eleven years old, but she stuffed Kleenex inside the bras that she didn't really need yet but wore on a regular basis. She gave me a bra to put on and ten sheets of Kleenex to go with it, but after I put it on, I started laughing and took it off again. She kept hers on and put on a soft brown-and-white-striped sweater that showed off her curves to anyone who cared to look. And she got looks. I don't know if she made the same offer of a bra and Kleenex to Karen, but it didn't matter. It didn't look like Karen took her up on it either if the offer was ever made.

So when we were getting ready to go to the Shrine Circus, I was glad that it was chilly enough to wear jackets, so the sex queen wouldn't have to be showing off and could just walk along with Karen and me to the bus stop. The sun was shining and we all three kept looking at our reflections in the store windows as we passed by them. Our hair was the most interesting thing to all of us that day, because every once in a while we would lift our heads and toss our hair a couple of times, just to see the sun reflect the bouncing shine back. It felt good to hear a couple of wolf whistles as we walked, even though I knew that those whistles were meant for Sherry. It's not that Karen and I were ugly or anything; it's just that Sherry was extremely pretty.

So we got on the bus and rode to the curling club, where the Shrine Circus was performing. As we walked into the building, we could smell popcorn and animals. We spotted the stall where they had those little monkeys on the sticks right away, but we only stopped to look and didn't buy any. Not yet. We had to see what else we could buy, then maybe we would get the monkey on the stick. I loved that little animal, all soft and fluffy, and with so many colors to choose from, but as soon as you shook them to make them dance, the elastic that attached them to the stick would usually break, and there you would be with just a monkey and a stick, instead of a monkey on a stick.

We got one pink cotton candy, just one for the three of us, and went to find seats. We could already see beautiful ladies in their sparkling swimsuits and net stockings and satin capes walking around in the entryways. The men wore tights in colors that matched the ladies' outfits, so you could tell who would be swinging with whom. There were crimson red glitter, royal blue sequin, bright yellow satin, pure white rhinestone, red-orange flame, and royal purple with ermine trim. Other combinations kept my eyes busy categorizing colors and defining sparkles as the performers appeared and the emcee directed our attention to ring number one, the center ring, and ring number three. I wondered why the center ring was not called "ring number two" but let the thought pass and kept looking at the ring that featured the spotlight at the moment.

We saw tiny dogs parading in on their hind legs, all dressed up in tutus and sparkles and ready to follow their trainer to their little stools and wait for their commands to turn somersaults, dance, or push each other in little red wagons. In another ring, little monkeys were waiting to do those same things. But in the center ring, tigers were snarling and acting tough when the guy with the whip wanted them to do their tricks. Crack! Crack! He flicked his whip in their direction and aimed the legs of his stool at them. One cat swiped at the whip with his huge paw both times, then jumped off his stool and ran to the ring of fire that he was supposed to jump through. One giant bound and he was through that ring without a singed hair! I saw the trainer toss a tidbit at the tiger and thought that the ferocity must be a part of the act.

Sherry was watching all of the sparkly ladies. Her eyes were shining, and her face looked like an angel. Karen was busy eating popcorn and looking here and there, not seeming particularly fascinated with anything but not looking bored either.

When we went outside to catch the bus home, it was still light out. It seemed like a different world. Cars were going by, people were walking in bunches, little kids were holding balloons or pointing at the sky and crying as their balloons floated away, and I was thinking about that pretty little bright-red monkey on a stick that I didn't get. Sherry was busy pulling her hair up into a ponytail like the ladies in the circus and Karen was looking at Sherry with suddenly skinny eyes. "Will you quit fooling with your hair? You think you're so hot!"

Sherry kept pulling her hair higher and higher on the back of her head, and her chin was pushing against her neck holding a rubber band intact, because she needed one hand to comb and one to guide the formation of the ponytail. She kept up her activity, pausing only briefly to look sideways at Karen, but she didn't say anything. She had her lips pursed together around two bobby pins. Finally, she secured her ponytail, put the bobby pins away, and gave her head a toss as she looked squarely at Karen. "I'm going to be a circus star!" Sherry announced. Karen snorted and turned in her seat to look out the window.

It wasn't a long ride home, but it seemed like it. Sherry and Karen had not said another word to each other the rest of the trip. I knew something was wrong, but I couldn't quite put my finger on what it was. Sherry and Karen were neighbors and saw each other more often than I saw either of them, so I thought they must be good friends. They certainly dressed alike, even though Sherry's clothes always seemed to look better on her than Karen's looked on Karen. I didn't even bother to try to dress like them, because it took money to do that, and that's one thing I didn't have. We had a big family and only rarely was anything I wore not a hand-me-down or secondhand item. I knew I would never be a fashion plate. I didn't want to be a circus lady either, but it was fun to watch them. We were nearly home, so I thought I'd better say something to them. "I sure liked all the bright colors and sparkly things the circus ladies were wearing!" Sherry's eyes sparkled, and Karen jerked her face away from the window and turned in my direction, frowning.

"They're stupid, and they're all just a bunch of whores! Did you see all of that makeup they were wearing? And those *ponytails*! You know what's under a pony's tail, don't you?" She looked directly at Sherry. Both girls' cheeks were bright red. We were off the bus by the time the last words were spoken, and we were two buildings away from Sherry's apartment. We walked in that direction as Sherry and Karen glared at each other. Sherry said, "Yeah, I know what's under *this* ponytail . . . *brains*, which is something you'll never have!"

Karen kept walking right past the entrance to Sherry's apartment building, which is where we were supposed to go after the circus. "Karen," I called, "Come back. Here's Sherry's mother coming to meet us." Karen kept walking. There was a wide expanse of lawn next door and stairs leading to the next building, which was set way back from the street. The lawn sloped down as far as the stairs went, then it evened out into a flat carpet of grass.

Karen looked back at me. "I'm not going into that little whore's house! I have too much *brains* to do that!" Sherry ran straight past me at Karen and tackled her. Down the slope they tumbled, Sherry holding Karen's arms pinned and Karen kicking at Sherry's shins in an attempt to free herself. It worked. Sherry let go, then grabbed a new hold on Karen's hair. Karen grabbed for Sherry's ponytail and pulled it with one hand while trying to undo the rubber band with the other.

I stood where I was and watched all of this as if it were in slow motion. I saw Sherry's mother come running down the steps of the apartment building and toward me. I stepped back and let her pass as she ran to where the girls were struggling with each other. She didn't bother to use

the steps but ran straight down the slope in the lawn, calling Sherry's name as she ran. "Sherry. Sherry. *Sherry!*" But
the fight didn't stop until Sherry's mother physically pulled
the girls apart and held them off from each other. She had
on her stern mother face and looked them both over before
she told Karen to go home. "I'm going to call your mother,"
she said.

Karen turned and ran toward the avenue that would
take her up the hill and home. "As for you, young lady," she
said to Sherry, pulling her by the ear toward the apartment,
"you're grounded." I stood, not knowing what to do. I hadn't
been sent home, but I hadn't been invited inside either. "Bye,
Sherry. Bye, Mrs. G.," I said. I decided the best thing to do
was to go home. Sherry usually walked me part of the way,
but this time I thought I'd better just get going. I lived a little
more than a mile away, but it was all city walking, so I figured
I'd be okay. "Do you want to come in and call your dad to
come and get you?" Mrs. G. asked. "No, I like to walk," I said,
not wanting to say that my dad was not home and wouldn't
come to get me anyway. We had lots of kids, not just one. Not
like Sherry, who was the main kid focus in her household.
I often doubted that my parents even knew whether I was
there. So I got to be pretty self-sufficient, I thought.

I walked home thinking about the events of the day.
I really liked going to the circus and all of the bright lights
and colors and sparkles. But I knew that was not the life
I wanted every day. It was just a diversion. Not enough to
fight or lose a friend over. I thought of the three long-haired
beauties and about how they would never be together again
after today.

Years later, Sherry moved away, "ran away to join the
circus," her mother said. Sherry was fifteen when she left to

find her dream. I remembered the auburn ponytail shimmering in the sunlight. I imagined that beautiful hair flying behind a gorgeous girl with sparkling green eyes high up on a trapeze in the center ring.

## I PREDICT RAIN

IT WAS ONE OF THOSE YELLOW DAYS. I just knew something was going to happen. It was too yellow to fight with my brothers or walk across the street to play paper dolls with my brother's girlfriend. I liked to call her that because it wasn't true, and it was always an effective way to start a fight. Actually, I liked her brother, and everybody knew it, but going over there to play paper dolls was a safe way to save face. Besides, she had a good assortment of dolls and cutout clothes, and sometimes we traced them to make our own designs. I guess I'm getting too old for dolls, but I'm ten and Ellen is nine, so I always say she wants to play, and what can I do? If I don't play with her and her paper dolls, she might cry.

She's good at crying on cue. Once, when her brother and his gang locked us up under her porch, I told her to call her brother and tell him she was going to tell their mom if he didn't let us out. He started laughing and saying, "Go ahead and tell!" until I told her to say it again, only this time pretend you're crying. It stunk under there, it was dark and smelled like old earth, and I just knew there were spiders and angleworms in there with us. Ellen called, "Bobby, I'm telling *Dad,*" as she put a wiggle in her voice, then followed up by making sobbing sounds. "Ahnnh-hanhh-hanhh-hanhh!" That worked, probably not so much the sobbing sounds as the more meaningful threat to tell Dad. Their dad was an old-fashioned kind of guy who thought guys were supposed to take care of girls and girls were supposed to do the dishes. They were not supposed to be locked up under the porch, especially not by their own brothers.

So Bobby gave in. "All right, quit your bawling! But just you. Get next to the door and tell me when you're there." Oh, great! He intends to keep me locked up in here. A new plan, quick, I thought to myself. "Okay, Ellie, here's what I want you to do," I whispered urgently in her ear. "Now listen! When they get ready to let you out, push hard on the door and don't let them close it. Stay in the way, so they can't close it! I'll get out first, then you can come. Okay?" She nodded.

Outside, Bobby was waiting with his friends. "Ellen, what's taking you so long? I thought you wanted to get out. Are you at the door?"

"Yes, I'm here."

"Okay, you can come out. But only you." The door opened about six inches as Bobby's face appeared to check to see that it was Ellen waiting to come out. "Let me out!" she yelled, as her brother opened the door a bit more. She shoved her shoulder against the door hard, at the same time I did, and it swung wide open, knocking her brother in the dirt. I jammed my way outside, and one of his friends grabbed me from behind and tried to pin my arms at my sides to push me back under the porch. Ellen watched and got scared. She really started crying and howling, no prompting required.

Her brother got up fast, dusting himself off. "Let her go, Joey," he ordered his sidekick. But Joey kept trying to hold on to me, Ellen kept howling, and I was mad as a wet hen. I jerked my elbow back as hard as I could, and old Joey doubled over holding his stomach. I took two steps toward him, and he straightened up as best he could and started running. I chased him for half a block as he ran toward his house, looking back only once to see if I was gaining on him. I let him go. I wasn't as strong as he was, and I knew it. What would I do if I caught him? Besides, I had to go back and see how Ellen was doing.

Ellen was inside washing her face when I got back. Bobby was sitting at the table reading a copy of a car magazine and sipping coffee. Oh, he's acting big, I thought. Just wait until his dad gets home and finds out what he did to Ellen and me! And I bet he doesn't even like that coffee that he's drinking!

"Ellie, I've got to go. The day is getting too yellow, and I think there's a storm on the way. Can you feel it in the air?"

"No, I can't feel anything except for how my arm hurts from pushing on that door. Bobby's really gonna get it when Dad gets home!"

Bobby didn't bother looking up.

"See you later, Ellie. Next time, bring your stuff over to my house instead." I walked quickly out the door and ran across the street to my front porch. It was a full-length porch, filling the whole width of the front of the house. I walked from one end of the porch to the other, surveying the air and feeling the hot, still, humid yellowness of the day. My brother came out the front door and looked at me. I looked up in the sky once more and felt inclined to make my announcement to him.

He was still just standing there, looking at me. I supposed I looked like heck, like I had been locked up under a porch somewhere and had to fight my way out, but I wasn't going to tell him the story. Let him look at my dirty face and hands and my tangled hair and wonder what I was up to. My cheeks still felt hot from the physical exertion I had just put myself through, so I guess they must have been nice and rosy.

The sight I presented at the precise moment I made my announcement must have been a formidable combination with the words that I delivered in as hollow a voice as I could manage. I lifted my arms skyward, outstretched, with palms up, as I stated, "I PREDICT RAIN!!" At my last word, a terrific bolt of lightning split the sky, followed by a very loud, rolling clap of thunder. The skies opened, and there was an immediate downpouring of rain.

My brother looked at me, his eyes wild as he took in the aftermath of my prediction. "WITCH!" he shouted, as he ran back in the house and slammed the door.

I looked at the pounding rain for a minute, amazed at the timing of the downpour, then went inside to glare at my brother as menacingly as I could.

## PETITIONS FOR GOOD HEALTH

MOM WAS A DARN GOOD NURSE. She was also a believer in the "Indian Way" of ensuring good health. I suppose I was about ten years old when Mom led me down the steps to the basement. We had an incinerator down there. I was sick at the time, so I was wearing pajamas and heavy socks. I descended the stairs carefully and followed Mom. She made her way over to the incinerator and opened the door. A fire was already burning, so I knew she had thought about making the trip downstairs with me. She handed me a little loose tobacco and kept a little in her own hand as she instructed me in making an offering and saying a prayer for good health. She said, "Primo will take care of you if you ask right." I wondered who Primo was but didn't ask. I said the prayer and sprinkled the tobacco into the fire, then watched as Mom did the same. We didn't talk anymore, just watched the fire burn for two or three minutes. Then we went back upstairs.

Mom was a bit of a puzzle to me. She studied nursing and went to work in the local hospital, but she also believed in and used traditional Native medicine in traditional ways. We drank something called swamp tea to keep us feeling strong and healthy. It was very tasty, and one of my sisters says she drank swamp tea, or ironwood tea, out of her bottle as a baby because she couldn't tolerate milk.

When Mom was a girl, she liked to be outside in the summertime. She said she spent a lot of time lying down with her head on a special rock, looking up at the clouds and sky. She used to go out there all the time. "That rock was a magnet to me, really." The rock is not there anymore. It got pushed off into the woods.

Both Mom and Grandma told me things that they had not told anyone else. And they both gave the same reason for not talking about their experiences. "No one would believe it and people would think I was crazy." I knew they weren't crazy, and I also knew that they were both wise. When they told me of certain experiences, I was fascinated, and they were both exceptionally gifted.

Mom certainly had a special kind of insight or foresight or premonition of events, especially those that involved our immediate family. Grandma told me that Mom was born with a veil over her face and that all of the elders from the village had come to see her when she was a baby. They thought the veil meant that mom would be gifted with special powers, that she was blessed. Now mothers tell their children that they have eyes in the backs of their heads when their children ask them how they know something. Mom never had to tell us that. We knew that whatever was going on with us, Mom would know. Distance meant nothing. Once, while we were living in California, Mom started walking around from room to room, opening and closing doors and appearing very restless. Finally, she said, "Something's wrong with your sister." She called family back in Minnesota to find that my sister had just been hospitalized.

Yep, Mom was a darn good nurse. And she didn't hold a grudge or let personal feelings interfere with her job. One time, while driving in Duluth, her car nearly collided with another one. The other driver rolled down his window and yelled at her, "Why don't you go back to the reservation?" She just kept driving and didn't reply to his question. Later, in her job as an emergency room nurse, she was called on to assist in emergency surgery on a patient. She did her job and the patient survived. The doctor who had done the surgery was relieved when the operation was complete. Only then did my mother look at him and say, "Well, now, doctor, what would you have done if I had gone back to the reservation?" Then she walked away.

As much as Mom believed in Native medicine and medical training, she was a lifelong believer in the power of prayer. She attended St. Mary's Catholic Church across the street from the hospital fairly often during the week and signed the family up as parishioners at Sacred Heart Catholic Church, both in Duluth. This powerful belief combination served her well, especially toward the end of her life.

She retired from her nursing career in Louisiana, where she had settled and lived for about thirty years.

In 1996, my siblings and I traveled from the northern states to be with her for bypass surgery. Mom knew so well what was happening to her body because of her medical training. Two of my siblings were also nurses, so we thought we had a pretty fair chance of understanding what mom's prognosis was. As it turned out, other resources seemed to come into play that even the doctor had not anticipated. Mom lived another five years beyond the night her doctor called the family together in the ICU after the surgery and told us she wouldn't make it through the night. We all went in and formed a circle around her bedside. Later, she said she vaguely remembered us all coming in to see her. She saw us circle her. She later said that before we came in, she felt like a magnet was pulling at her from all directions. Nobody said anything at the time. We joined hands and we all looked at her as she lay in bed looking around at each of us and not saying anything. We stayed in the circle for about a half an hour. Then we went back to the waiting room.

Dr. Hamm told her that after we left the room, he didn't know what had happened, but all of her vital signs had suddenly returned to normal. He said he couldn't explain what had happened. He said, "If you believe in miracles, then this is a miracle." This is also what he told us when he came to the family waiting area after he had talked to Mom. Another of Mom's doctors, Dr. McAllister, asked her if she prays. She told him she prayed all the time.

I think of Mom's petitions for good health every time I lay my tobacco down. A prayer is a prayer, and our Creator is listening, no matter where we are when we send up that petition.

# Fond du Lac

WHEN I WAS A KID, seven or eight years old, my playground was out behind Grandma's little shack, right beside the garden, in a big dirt hole. Boy, did I have fun. Sometimes Gram would let me take a real cup, spoon, and saucer out in the big hole with me. The cup and saucer were metal, white with a black rim. The spoon was an ordinary teaspoon. With the cup, I could get water from the rain barrel or from the bucket in the kitchen and carry it back to the big hole. The hole was about six or eight feet from the back of the house, so when Gram looked out the window she could see me. Or if she was working in the garden, she could look up and see me, or if she was hanging clothes out on the line, she could turn around and see me. Or if she was walking to or from the outhouse, she could see me. I concluded that's why the big hole was placed where it was. I could be seen at all times.

The hole was about five feet across and two feet deep. In the summer, there was no need to use it for "dancing on rice," as Dad called it, when he was jigging rice after the wild rice harvest. I got to claim the dig as my own during the warm weather. The dirt from the hole didn't go to waste either. My dad used it when he needed dirt to bank the house. That way, when winter came, we were protected from the draft that might have come in from around the floor of the little tar paper shack that Grandma and I called home.

Grandma's home in winter. She loved her "little palace," as she called it. Although small, it was filled with love, and she preferred living there to anywhere else.

I loved my winter home with Grandma, and in the summer I loved my little outdoor dirt hole home, too. There I was in my own little world. This was my house, and the bugs and beetles that came in were my guests. They liked certain types of grass stalks, so I took little trips to the fields to gather the kinds that would bring the prettiest insects into the hole. While they dined on the grass stalks, I would be busy stirring my water and mud in the saucer to make the daintiest little cakes I could imagine. They were very tiny, very delicate, with little bitty floral and green trim. They could be any shape, depending on how stiff I made the batter and how I used my fingers to shape the cakes. I could pinch them, or swirl them, or roll them into cylinders. And I could use different flowers to add color to my cakes.

Nature provided the fields around our shack with all colors of wildflowers: white daisies with yellow centers, purple bell-shaped flowers with yellow trim, sweet-smelling pink roses with ruffled petals, stiff bright-orange Indian paintbrushes, as my dad called them, and lavender, rose, and white clover. The tall grasses that had developed seed at the tops were put into my kid cuisine also. I thought the seeds looked like rice, and I could pretend they were coconut on my cakes. If I put petals into the mud, it would change color. Not much, but enough to notice. I did like to put all the tiniest flowers and buds on the tops of my cakes. It was wonderful to decorate two or three cakes and set them on the ledge of the big hole, then watch while bees and butterflies would come by to pay them compliments.

On a warm day, I could lie for hours at the bottom of my big hole and watch the bugs and beetles and bumblebees and butterflies add to the colorful display of wildflowers and mud pies. I even had shelves in the walls of my big hole, because I wanted a place to set the pies in case it rained. They were indented into the wall and offered protection from a gentle rain, but a good downpour would cause the cakes to become part of the big hole itself, which was okay because that's where they came from anyway.

I was about eight years old when this corner of the world was my domain, but I never lost my fascination with texture, color, design, wildlife, and wildflowers. The smell of the fields after a gentle rain was a little piece of heaven to me. I knew that all life needed this water to survive, and I thanked the Great Spirit for all of these wonderful gifts every time. *Chi Miigwech, Chi Manitou.*

I used to think about what it must have been like when there were only Indians in this land. How playing with mud pies and wildflowers must have been the thing to do back then and playing with sticks and stones was not thought to be odd. I had stones that I would bring into my big hole, but I usually kept the stones in the lean-to in front of the house. I didn't want them to get lost, so I kept them in a coffee can and out of the rain, so the can wouldn't rust and leak the rust on the stones. If I did bring the stones into the big hole, though, they would be placed on my metal saucer in water. Being in water brought out the color in them, especially when the sun shined directly on them. They weren't all agates, but the majority were. Others just turned unusual colors when they were wet.

How much did I treasure these rocks and stones? They must have meant a great deal to me because sixty years have passed since I found them, and I still have them, along with more that I have found since then.

The big hole is still there, sort of. It is merely a lumpy indent now because someone tried to fill it up. There's not a little girl there anymore to make wonderful pies and cakes

Grandma watched as I played in the big dirt hole behind the house, and she saw me make mud pies with water, mud, and flower petals. One day, she brought me a saucer and spoon. My pie creations became more elaborate, with agates embellishing the perimeter of the pie. My insect neighbors loved it!

and bask in the sunlight watching yellow butterflies and pink, yellow, white, purple, and orange wildflowers. But all of these things still live in my heart, along with the old woman who gave me a cup, a saucer, and a spoon as though these were the greatest treasures I would ever receive.

GRAM ALWAYS HAD A GARDEN in the summer, and she planted, weeded, hauled water to it, and harvested it until she was in her late sixties or early seventies. I remember her teaching me how to plant carrots and radishes when I was eight years old. She made the little mounds of earth and hollowed out a half-inch row along the top of the mound to drop seeds into. She handed me a handful of seeds and said, "Here. Now you plant these, sprinkling them along the way you do with salt." So I took the seeds and sprinkled them out the way I did when I seasoned my food with salt. I liked salt on my food, so I planted the carrot seeds in generous sprinkles. When it came time to go and thin the plants, Gram looked at my work and called me over to her for another lesson. "Look, here, Janis, these carrots are all coming up in one spot with nothing growing in between. Did you sprinkle the seeds like salt?" I said yes and showed her the movement of my hand as I had planted the seeds earlier in the season. She laughed a hearty laugh and said, "You must like salt." Then she showed me how to thin the plants and how to sprinkle the next batch of seeds, which were radishes. We planted radishes more often than carrots each year because they grew faster. We also had potatoes, corn, tomatoes, cucumbers, and onions in the garden.

I watched her hoe the garden and gather up the weeds in between each harvest. Watching her out there in the garden with the trees as a background gave me a peaceful feeling, as though there were only she and I and the earth and trees and sky. She was very deliberate in her movements, careful not to hoe the plants and telling me not to kill the ladybugs that landed on the potato plant leaves. It was so quiet out in the country; we could hear the birds singing and the trees whooshing their leaves together when the wind blew.

She had guys who would come over and clear the fields and brush for her sometimes, and then we would get to eat those fresh vegetables, because she always cooked for her helpers. We had a table set up outside under the shade of the big tree that grew in front of our little shack. It was like having a picnic every day during the summer. We had an oilcloth table cover that made a pretty background to our dishes. Sometimes I would pick a bouquet of wildflowers and put them in water in a canning jar in the center of the table, but not often, because I liked to see the flowers in the fields where they belonged or as garnish on my mud pies when I was entertaining insects and butterflies, as I did when I played in the big hole behind our house.

Gram had a woodstove outside in a lean-to where she cooked in the summer, to keep it cool in the house. We had fresh fried potatoes (*opiniig*, she called them), fried sunfish, cut-up onions, tomatoes, and cucumbers. Wah! Those guys liked her cooking! Me, too. She never had trouble getting helpers to clear the fields for her. She paid them a little, too, but they liked her cooking the best.

Sitting outside was a terrific way to spend time. Butter-flies were everywhere and wildflowers in all colors grew nearby. How I loved looking at the wild roses in shades of pink, and the different purple, white, yellow, and orange flowers of all different shapes and sizes. Even the dandelions were beautiful to behold, both in their yellow stage and in their white gone-to-fluff stage. After a gardening session, we would have hot tea and a buttered biscuit or sometimes a cookie. One special trip to town included Gram buying matching straw hats for us to wear while we worked in the garden. We needed hats because we didn't hurry through the gardening chores. Without the protection from the sun, our skin, though dark, would have burned. I can still see the garden scene, with Grandma out there in a flowered print dress, long cotton stockings, and sensible shoes, a straw hat, and sometimes a loose-fitting sweater with pockets for a handkerchief, and the ever-present hoe. There was no place else in the world I'd rather be than watching the sugar bush baby caress the earth, coaxing the Creator's gifts to come forward.

## WASH DAYS

ON THE RESERVATION, when it was time to do laundry, Gram and I did it outside. There was an early method of washing clothes and a later method, after we got a washing machine. Both methods were done outside, and neither method involved electricity. This was in the 1950s and 1960s, before Gram got a new house with electricity, built for her by the tribe. She didn't like the new house and never got an electric washing machine, even when she had an electric hook-up for it. Later, after she got indoor plumbing, it was easier to get water, but in the old days we had two methods of getting water. The early method was to get a couple of buckets and walk to a neighbor's house to fetch it from their pump, or to use what had accumulated in the rain barrel beside the house. We also sometimes walked to the lake to dip it out and haul it back up to the laundry location. We had a clothesline strung between two large trees. The line was propped up by a long tree branch with a fork in it to hold up the line at the midway point.

Before we got the washing machine, which was powered by a small motor attached to it, we did all of the laundry in a washtub on the grass outside the front door. That made it easier to haul the heated water from the woodstove to the tub. We used a plunger and scrub board to clean the clothes. A good bar of Fels-Naptha would be employed to scrub heavily soiled clothing against the scrub board. General laundry was simply placed in the water and plunged up and down by hand with a device that had a long wooden handle and a metal cone-shaped head attached to it. After washing our items, we handwrung them and placed them in a separate basin next to the washtub. We carried the soapy water in the washtub to the tall grasses in the field and dumped it out. Then we placed rinse water in the same washtub, dunked our clothes to rinse them, then handwrung them again. Finally, we carried the clean clothes in a basin to the clothesline to hang them up. We used clothespins and attached the laundry to the long clothesline to swing in the outdoor breezes to dry. It smelled so fresh when it was done! No fabric softeners were needed to make clothes smell good. When laundry is dried outside, sun-kissed and wind-whipped, that's one of the freshest smells the Creator gave us.

While we were doing the laundry, we had time to visit and tell each other stories. Gram always wanted to know what I saw on my walks to the road or to the mailbox. And as I grew older, she wanted more detail. I remember starting out as a youngster telling her that I had seen a bird, or a tree, or a flower, or an insect. She would ask questions about it. Where did I see it, what was it doing (even trees and flowers), what color was it? As I grew older I added more detail to the stories before she asked me. I learned that it's important to know what's going on around you. It's important to recognize that trees and flowers "do things" too, not just birds and insects. It's important to really look at things and recognize likenesses and differences. I learned early the difference between a robin and a crow, an oak and a maple, a wild rose and a lady slipper. She taught me the difference between "bird berries" and "snake berries" (those we could not eat) and June berries and blueberries, those delicious berries we could eat. The ones she called snake berries looked an awful lot like blueberries, so I'm glad she told me the difference. I could also tell the difference between the sound of an owl and the sound of a bear outside at night.

Gram liked to tell stories about owls and bears. She told me one story about an owl who watched what children do. She said the owl always knows if you're not clean enough and will come at night to say "Who, whoo, *whoooo* . . . 's got dirty knees?" I always made sure I washed myself clean, so the owl wouldn't have to come and ask me that.

Another owl story involved a lesson that she passed on to one of her sons about not making fun of people. There was an old man who used to walk around the reservation, and as he got older he began to wear glasses. The older he got, the thicker the glasses were, until one day Gram's son saw the old man coming and said, "Run and hide! Here comes gookooko'oo!!" (That's the sound of the Indian word that means owl.) Well, Gram heard him say it and she scolded him right away. "Don't you make fun of that old man!

He can't help it that he has to wear glasses to see! If you make fun of him, someday you won't be able to see so good yourself!"

The story about the bear was just a tale of precaution. If we're out in the woods, and we hear a bear, move away from the sound as fast as you can but try not to run. The bear might think you're after him, or if it's a mother bear, she might be more dangerous than the male bear, especially if she has cubs. Sometimes bears came pretty close to the shack at night, and I could hear their deep moan-like grunts. They did sound like hoot owls, but they were a bit raspier. We didn't live far from the dump ground, which was three miles away, so bears were more likely to go there than to visit us. But on occasion, at night, they did.

We always did our mending on wash day, too. Gram liked to say, "You might be poor, but you don't have to be dirty or raggedy." She had a big button can that she kept handy for replacing buttons and snaps. Besides the functional buttons, though, she also had a good assortment of old buttons in the can from wornout garments. I loved looking at those buttons—just never got tired of looking at them. They were various shapes and colors and had rhinestones in them. When we were working outside, the stones picked up the sun's rays and cast shimmers of light on the things around us. Gram allowed me to play with the buttons for a while and then would give me little chores to do. "Many hands make light work" was another one of her sayings.

We were always busy, but it didn't feel like work. I just loved spending time with Grandma. She wasn't what you could call lazy, not by any stretch of the imagination. She believed in work and in "moving your bones." She usually got things she needed for herself, but sometimes, when she had a lapful of mending to do, she would ask me to get the scissors or thimble or thread for her. Sometimes I couldn't find the item she needed. She knew where everything was and, besides that, Gram could usually see much better than I could any detail around us. So she would direct me to the spot the needed item was located. If I couldn't find it, she would direct me again.

I recall only one time that she grew impatient with me for not being able to see what she was telling me to bring her. She needed a thimble, and I couldn't see it. "It's over there on the shelf," she said. I looked at the shelf above the table but could not see the thimble.

"Where, Gram? I don't see it."

"It's right there on the shelf," she said again, pursing her lips to point in the direction of the thimble. I walked over to where she was sitting and put my head beside hers, trying to see where she was looking. Suddenly, she turned her head in my direction, put her finger below her eye, and pulled her eyelid down, saying, "Look here in my eye!"

"Oh, Gram!" I responded, laughing. I went back to the shelf, moved the Big Ben clock that she kept there, and found the thimble.

Thereafter, when I couldn't find something, I would go to the mirror, pull down my eyelid, and say, "Look here in my eye!" That still makes me laugh when I think about it, especially because my eyes look so much like Grandma's. It's a little technique I use when I get to missing her too much, because it brings her right back, sense of humor and all.

On wash day, if we had finished the mending, we embroidered pillowcases to pass the time while we waited for laundry to dry. Then Gram would crochet the opening of the cases and make fancy lace edges on them. One time she embroidered a deep pink ribbon on one case and a red ribbon on the other case. I noticed the difference in color but didn't say anything until after she finished the work. Then I commented that I liked both colors. She picked them up and held them side by side. "Oh, Yiii, Jaa'iins!! Why didn't you tell me I was using two different colors?"

"Oh, Gram, I thought you knew! Those are both really pretty colors, so I hope you leave them like that." She did.

One time Gram tried to teach me to knit. She had yarn that was the color of fresh garden peas, and she was making a potholder. I got a chair and sat down next to her, watching her work. She was always so calm and unhurried; it was restful just being around her, even when she was working. She spoke in a soft voice and sometimes used unusual words. It always thrilled me to hear the way she expressed herself. She said words like "'tisn't" for "it isn't" and "'tis" for "it is," which made it fun just hearing her talk.

After I watched her knit for a while, listening to her explain what she was doing with the yarn and the knitting needles, she reached into her yarn sack and handed me a pair of knitting needles and a ball of yarn. "You can make a potholder, too, Jaa'iins. 'Tisn't hard," she said. I got the yarn started, then slowly knit-purled my way through the number of stitches she told me to make before turning my needles to go in the other direction for the second row. We worked slowly, leisurely, sitting outside enjoying the day and each other's company, sometimes talking, sometimes not, waiting for the laundry to dry. We took a little tea break, then continued knitting until the potholders were done. We ended up with two potholders that were both the same color yarn.

There the similarity ended. My potholder was about a five-inch square and fairly firm, while Gram's was a good seven-inch square and quite soft. I was already ten years old, too old to cry over something like that, but I sure felt like crying. "It's too small," I told Gram. "It doesn't look like yours!" I had tried to be careful, to not drop any stitches and to make sure the yarn would hold together, but it was just so small! Gram took my potholder in both hands, held it up, and looked at the work, then laid it down on top of hers. "That's just right to put a hot dish on," she said. "You knit tighter than I do, that's all. If you add more stitches to your rows, the potholder will be bigger. Or if you don't pull the yarn as tight, the knit will be bigger, like mine. You did good." She always found something good to say. She put little loops on our potholders and hung them in the kitchen side by side.

Gram thought it was important to be honest, too, and told me a story about her mother teaching her a lesson. We were picking through the spools of thread in her sewing box, when I pulled out a little spool, smaller than the rest; it had bright red thread on it. As red is one of my favorite colors, I told her how pretty I thought that spool of thread was. She took it from my hand, held it for a minute, and then handed it back to me. I could always tell when she was going to tell me a story, and I knew from the way she gazed over my head off into space that a story was coming.

Sure enough. Gram told me about one time when she was a girl and had gone visiting a neighbor with her mother. Shortly after they got home from the visit, Gram started playing with a little spool of thread. Her mother asked her where she got it. Gram said she didn't want to tell her mother that she had picked it up from the table at the neighbor's house, but she told her anyway. "I must have been six years old at that time, and my mother made me take the thread back," Gram said. "My mother told me, 'Don't you ever pick up anything that doesn't belong to you. That's not your thread!' Well, it was a long walk back to that neighbor's house, but my mother took me back that same day to return the thread and tell the neighbor what I did. I never forgot that," Gram said. "After that, I wouldn't pick up anything that didn't belong to me. Not hairpins, or ribbons, or even rubber bands. If it wasn't mine, I didn't pick it up."

That was one story I never forgot either, and I've tried to instruct my son and grandchildren with the same lesson. If it isn't yours, don't take it.

We usually started our laundry early in the morning, just as soon as the dew was gone from the grass. We finished it the same day and had fresh-smelling clothing and linens until the next wash day.

After dad brought us the motor-run washing machine, there wasn't a marked difference in our routine. It was a little faster, but noisier with the motor running. Also, having a hand-cranked wringer attached to the machine made the wringing process faster. But there are trade-offs for speed. The motor noise was something that I didn't like. I couldn't hear the birds singing over the racket, and Gram and I had to wait to talk to each other. Birdsong and Gram's voice were two of my favorite sounds back then, so it was a shame to have to lose even a little bit of either one in the name of "progress." Country memories like this just cannot be improved.

## A Powwow at the Fairgrounds

It was late August 1958, when Deer River, Minnesota, held the wild rice festival to celebrate the harvest of wild rice for the Chippewa Indians and to put up a carnival and make money for the storekeepers in town from all the people who would come. That's the American way.

My cousins, my brother, and I danced at the powwow. Afterward the adults gave us a dollar in change so we could go on the carnival rides. I never carried a purse when I was a kid, so everything I had went in my pockets. When I got off the Hammer, everything I had in my pockets was gone. I looked around at the base of the ride and found my coins and my comb. I vowed never to go on the Hammer ride again.

We walked down the fairway looking at all the prizes we could win if we could just get that nickel exactly on the circle for a lucky strike or if we could just toss that ring exactly around the neck of the Coke bottle. Not lopsided, that wouldn't count. It had to be around the Coke bottle's neck like a necklace. What about if we knocked down all the milk bottles that were in that pyramid shape with one of those softballs? It looks easy enough when the guy who runs the stand does it.

Ahead of me on the fairway, I spotted my friend Spud ambling toward us. He was not dressed for dancing, and I wondered why, as he was one of the best dancers I had ever seen. He just came for the rides or the games. He was pretty strong, so I asked him if he would try to knock down the milk bottles, but he said no, he had to get a beer. I looked at him to see if he was fooling. His eyes looked very bright, but red and skinny. Skinnier than usual, I mean, because his eyes had a natural slant to them. We must be related to the Asiatic people, I thought, before I asked Spud, "What do you mean, you have to get a beer? You're only twelve years old!" He put his hands in the pockets of his jacket and looked at me, a very slight smile on his face. "Well, I'm drunk, can't you tell?"

I looked at him more closely. I know what drunk looks like. And I don't believe it, but he's drunk all right. How did he get drunk?

We walked back to the end of the fairway where the pow-wow was going on. The drum was still set up in the center of the dance area, and dancers were still going strong. Oh, that drum sounds good! My uncle is the lead singer, and he has a powerful voice. People like to dance when he sings. I look at him. He's wearing his usual ballpark cap, with the bill tilted lopsided as usual. That was the way he liked to wear it. On anyone else it might look sloppy. On Uncle Ray, it just looked like Uncle Ray. My other uncle was there, too. He brought his family to dance.

The women in that family all wore jingle dresses, dark with bright-silver cone-shaped tins that were sewn so close together they made music when they touched each other. My aunt's dress was navy blue with jingle cones, one of my female cousins wore a blue velvet dress, another wore a black velvet dress, a third and a fourth cousin both wore black dresses, though not velvet, and all of the dresses were trimmed with the jingle cones and yellow and red ribbon. My male cousins wore brightly colored fancy dance outfits, and they were the main attraction to the tourists who stood around watching. My brother also wore dance regalia, but his was a chief's headdress of black and white feathers with turquoise trim. He was small and a tremendous dancer, so his dancing drew a crowd, too. My grandmother was there with us wearing her black jingle dress and beaded vest.

I looked around for Spud. Where did he go, anyway?! Darn him. He'd better not be looking for a beer! He wouldn't have a tough time finding one, I knew. He would look for cars that came to powwows but didn't hold dancers or singers, just lonely, disillusioned people who sat in the shadows listening to the drumming and drinking their beers. I imagined that they were thinking of the old days, when there was more to being an Indian than coming to a carnival to be a spectacle for the crowds. Only sometimes would I think that way. Other times, I would just go into the circle and dance and forget about anything else except the beat of the drum and the feeling of warmth that surrounded me when I looked at the faces of the other dancers. I loved the sounds of the big bells that the men wore as they blended with the soft tinkling of the jingle dress cones. The bright colors of the fancy dancers whirled around us, along with the more sedate colors and regal movements of the traditional male dancers. These were my people and I felt at peace among them.

Gram told me that we must dance carefully and keep our feet close to the ground. We should not try to dance fancy, like the boys. "Look at that one over there," she said sadly, pointing her lips in the direction of a young jingle dress dancer. I looked and saw that the girl was dancing in a style that strongly resembled "the bop," a popular rock-and-roll step of the fifties. "She wants to be a boy," Gram continued. "Don't you dance like that. You're an Indian girl, and Indian girls don't dance like that."

Years later, I had occasion to remember what Gram had said, because my brother wanted to learn how to bop. He's two years younger than I am, so I felt safe in trying to teach him something I wasn't so sure I was good at. My older sisters had taught me the step, so I told my brother to watch my feet and do what I was doing. He stood across from me and kept his head lowered as he watched my feet.

He hunched his shoulders in concentration, and his eyes looked sparkly. He's so darn smart, he learns things right away. He's already got the step down pat.

But he wasn't following me, and his vulture-like pose was about to make me laugh. If I laughed, he would quit, so we needed to do something different. "This isn't working too good," I told him. "Come over here and stand beside me. Let's try it that way." He came and stood at my left side.

"Now, do what I do." I touched my right toe to the floor, then brought my right foot down flat, followed by a step with the left toe and bringing my left foot down flat. We took about three steps like this, and he followed my every move. We went forward in unison perfectly. Then I looked over at him. He had his arms flexed at the elbow with his wrists and fingers drooping, and he was looking at me sideways, head tilted, with a big grin on his face. "This isn't the bop! This is the Indian dance!" he said laughing. I stopped short and joined him in his laughter, because he was right. We were dancing a step that in later years was called the intertribal, because all dancers, men, women, and children, danced to the music doing the same step. It was very reminiscent of the simple lady's jingle step my grandmother had taught me and told me to hang on to instead of trying to "dance like a boy." Well, Gram, we all dance alike sometimes, but at least we're all still dancing.

All except for old Spud, that is, who had gone looking for beer. Okay, I'm going to find him and make him get orange pop with me. I'm thirteen and I don't drink beer, why should he? Pop tastes better anyway. Maybe if he didn't live on the reservation, he wouldn't feel like he had to drink. But city Indians drink, too. Maybe if you're Indian, you're supposed to drink. Nah!

I found him sleeping in the back seat of his dad's car. He looked little and worn out. He was worn out, and when he wakes up he'll be sick. Well, for now he's okay. I'll find Gram and see if I can get something to eat. I want to dance some more, too, but it seemed like more fun when my strong, energetic, fancy dancing friend was dancing, too, and not sleeping it off in the car. Twelve years old. He said he started drinking when he was ten. How could I have missed that? The signs must have been there. I just wasn't expecting it in one so young.

## DANCING UP A STORM

WE TOOK THE GREYHOUND BUS to Cass Lake for the powwow. When we went there, we usually camped out-doors and enjoyed visiting and sharing food with other campers. Grandma liked what she called "good old-fashion Indian cooking," so there we were, camped out in the field by the powwow circle, waiting for the fish soup to be done. Gram peered into the kettle and watched the other lady stir the soup, sniffing the air at the good aroma. I wanted a bowl of soup, too, so I could get ready to go and dance. Finally, it was ready, and we ate. Gram chatted with the lady while I wandered around in the field, looking at plants and insects as I so often liked to do. It was summer and warm outside. I looked over toward the bleachers to see if there were any kids my age to play with while I waited. We should go dance soon, I thought. Gram looked up at me and said, "Okay, let's go dance." I jumped, wondering if I had said the words aloud. I didn't think I had, because I knew better than to interrupt adults when they were talking to each other.

Gram went into the nearby tent to change into her jingle dress. I loved to hear that tinkling sound as she maneuvered into the dress. She came back outside, jingle cones twinkling and sparkling in the sunlight. Her moccasins scuffed up a little dust as she walked toward me. She handed me a little bag to hold while she sat down to apply a little powder to her face. The shine on her nose disappeared under her powder puff. She reached for the bag I held, then stood up. I knew in just minutes we would start dancing. I rejoiced at the sound of the drumming and walked a little faster. "Jaa'iins, don't run. We're almost there!" Gram commanded.

I slowed my pace to match hers. "Sorry, Gram, I just want to dance."

"Me, too," she replied.

We got to the powwow circle and danced in. It felt so good to be stepping in time to the drumming. I watched Gram's footsteps for a while, then looked up so I could see her face. She always looked so regal when she danced. We danced slowly around the circle, and at one point she took my hand and moved me in a different direction from our original arc. I wondered why she had made the change but merely followed her lead without saying anything.

As we left the circle at the end of the dance, she leaned down and told me to look at her hand. I did. She had her hand cupped slightly as though she were holding something. Then she moved her hand ever so slightly with a back-and-forth movement, as though she was sprinkling something from it.

"If you see someone dancing close to you doing this, move away from them," she said.

I said okay and didn't ask why. She told me why later on that day.

We rested a while, danced some more, rested again, danced some more, then Gram said she was going to go back to the campsite to change out of her dress. It was time to eat again. I said I wanted to dance a while longer and then I would come back to the campsite. Gram agreed with the plan and headed back toward the tent. I watched her go, noting the direction carefully, then went back into the dance circle. I moved with the other dancers to the beat of the drum and listened as the men singers sang familiar songs to accompany their drumming. Halfway through the second song, the wind started to pick up. The singers continued singing. The dancers continued dancing. Suddenly as the song ended, the wind whipped up a cloud of dust. The dancers started to leave the circle, waiting for the dust cloud to settle. But the wind picked up and the dust cloud grew thicker and darker. The wind pelted the dancers with sand and the singers quickly got up and wrapped their drums to carry them out of the circle. Dancers and singers started running as the wind sent blinding clouds of dust everywhere. It was too dark to see anything, and I tried to think of which direction I should run to find Gram. She had no doubt reached the camp and was safe inside the tent.

Now I wished I had gone with her. Too late, I was stuck in the dust storm. I started pushing against the wind, walking as fast as I could in the direction of the camp, I thought. After walking for five minutes, I started to think I might be lost. I couldn't see anything and thought if I could just find a table or a chair, I could get under it for protection from the wind and dust storm. But I saw nothing.

Then I heard a faint voice calling my name. "Jaaa-nis. Jaaa-nis." The syllables rose and fell, but I recognized

Gram's voice and moved toward it. What was she doing out in this storm?

The voice got closer, and I called back, "Gram, Gram, I'm over here!"

"Jaaa-nis. Jaaa-nis." We continued to exchange signals until at last I saw a familiar figure taking shape amid the dust. I ran toward her, so thankful that she is there. She reached out to gather me into the folds of the blanket she carried around her shoulders. I was grateful for the protection from the stinging particles of dust, safe in Gram's arms and wrapped in the blanket. We walked as fast as we could back to the tent. Once inside, I told Gram that the storm came up so fast that everyone just scattered out and ran. She said she shouldn't have left me there, that sometimes those dancers who carry those powders are up to no good. "Next time," she told me, "when I come back to camp, you come with me."

Many traditional people believed in the power of Ojibwe medicine, both good and bad, and not all people rely on the good medicine. It wasn't long before the Cass Lake community no longer used the grounds for powwows but moved on to dance in another area. The fish soup was delicious wherever we went.

## SNARED RABBITS

I BET SOMEBODY THOUGHT I wrote "scared rabbits" at first! But no, you read it right. I'm going to tell you a little story about snared rabbits. It fits right in with a winter walk in the woods and a toboggan ride and two little girls going out with Grandma to pick greens to make wreaths. I'm not making this up. I got the story secondhand, but after I tell it to you, I'll add on a little one that I know about from first-hand experience.

So remember how we used to go for walks in the woods with Grandma in the winter when she was going to check her snares for rabbits? Yes, I remember those walks.

Well, this time Arleen and Pat, two of my older sisters, went with Grandma. Grandma really believed in bundling up for the winter weather. She was wearing that black thing that she used to wrap around her head like a turban. She never changed her style, and she passed it on to those of us who were wise enough to follow her good advice. "Dress for the weather," she always said. And she did as she said.

Arleen and Pat must have been bundled up, too, because Arleen said they walked across Grandma's little road and through the road and all the way back into the woods across the big road. That's got to be an efficient way because Grandma had forty acres, and it sounds like she took them to the back of the fortieth acre. Well, she was checking her snares and gathering princess pine for the Christmas wreaths that she made each year, so she brought a toboggan to carry all the goods back home. Arleen said that Grandma also wanted to take back any birch bark that they found loose in the woods because it was good kindling to start the fire.

Grandma's little tar paper shack had three rooms: a bedroom, packed to the ceiling with boxes of good stuff; a combination bedroom/sitting room/dining area; and a little bitty kitchen with enough room for a wood-burning cooking stove, a basin and stand for water, and three short shelves to put dishes on. In the combination bedroom/sitting room/dining area was another wood-burning stove that could heat the house and boil stuff that needed boiling.

Back to the walk in the woods we go. It was a bright, white, sparkly kind of day. Snow can cause a diamond sparkly effect in the country after a fresh snowfall where the beauty far surpasses that of any synthetic gem. They were finding princess pine for the wreaths, rabbits from the snares, and birch bark for the fire. Grandma let the girls take turns riding on the toboggan while she pulled it and the load through the snow. Finally, they were ready to head back home. Everything was piled on the toboggan. Grandma looked at the piled-up toboggan, looked at the girls, and suddenly she plopped down on the toboggan and started laughing. "Well, girls," she said, "I'm ready to go!" She handed them the rope.

The two little girls looked at each other, then at Grandma on the toboggan with the pile of stuff. Arleen said, "Holy cow! How are us two little girls going to pull all of that stuff?"

She couldn't remember if they really had to pull. Grandma was just fooling them. She would not have made little girls pull the load on the toboggan. I know that Grandma was fun and had a good sense of humor, especially when it came to those walks in the woods.

One time I was with her, just the two of us, and I was about eight years old. I was small, because Grandma was a shorty, and I was even shorter than she was. We were both dressed for the weather, as you might expect, and it's a good thing because what happened on the walk might not have been so funny if we hadn't been all bundled and layered up. The cold didn't bother us because we were dressed for it. We hadn't gotten far on our walk, just across Grandma's little road and onto the path toward the big road. It had snowed, so there was a thick blanket of snow on all the trees that made the branches hang low.

As Grandma went ahead of me, she picked up a big stick and used it to knock the snow off of the low hanging branches to make them light enough to lift out of our way. I loved to watch that fresh snow all sparkly like diamonds in the sunlight, then sifting to the ground like crystal sugar when Grandma swung her stick. So I picked up a stick to knock snow off, too. Only, being so small, I couldn't reach quite as high as Grandma could. I tried. I took a good high hop and swung hard at the branch in front of me. I missed the branch. That wouldn't have been so bad, but Grandma was in front of me. Whack! The stick came down hard on the back of her head. I saw her stop, bring her hand up to her head, and turn around to look at me all at the same time.

"Hoooo . . . hooooo . . . hoooooo, Janis!" she said, making the "hoooooo" sound high and spooky like a night owl. "You almost knocked me out!"

I was watching her reaction and listening to her words from the ground, where I was rolling around in the snow, laughing. "Oh, Grandma, I was just trying to knock the snow off the trees, like you were doing. I'm sorry! I missed and the stick landed on your head."

"Hooooo . . . hoooooo . . . hoooooo, I know it!" she said, rubbing her head. "You got to learn to be more careful."

It's not that I'm so mean. I was just a little kid, trying to do what the grownups do, and it didn't work. Grandma was a good one for learning lessons from, whether you were trying to learn or not. Things just happened that left an impression on you if you were lucky enough to spend time with her. I was extra lucky, because I remember so many episodes with her, like the time we went walking to the neighbor's house in the summer to get our buckets of water. But that's another story.

## PROPERTY RIGHTS

I COULDN'T SEE THE THINGS that Gram could see at a glance. I wore glasses from age six on, but not all the time. I don't recall wearing them at Big Lake. Gram didn't wear glasses until later in life, starting in her sixties. Maybe she needed them before then, but she never seemed to. She could see everything from great distances away. Sometimes she would tell me to look where she was looking to see if I could see what she was seeing. I usually could not.

Of course, she had lived on the property for forty years and often mentioned that my grandfather had built the house we lived in. That's why she never wanted to move out, even after the tribe built a new house for her that had running water and electricity. It was just across the road from

Grandma Cecelia Robinson (left) in front of her house in 1976 with Lucy Robinson (daughter-in-law), me, Joe Fairbanks (grandson), Earl Robinson (son, married to Lucy), and daughter Alvina Robinson Caldwell.

her old house, but she just kept living in her old house for as long as she could. Eventually, though, she did move into the new house, but she never did close up the old house. It was still standing after she walked on.

Living in one place for forty years is a big advantage to being able to tell when something is out of place. One time, it was very dark outside. Gram got up and peered out the front window. "There's something down there," she said, as she stared down the driveway toward the end of the road. I looked out and could see nothing but blackness. She turned the wick down on the lamp and told me to close my eyes, then look again. I did. Nothing. She was putting on her sweater and had put the flashlight on the table. Oh, no! We're going out there! I thought but said nothing. "Put your coat on. We're going to walk down there and see who's there," she said.

"What if it's a bear?" I inquired.

"It's not a bear. It's something shiny. Somebody is parked down there, and this is private property." So we walked to the end of the road. We were almost there before I saw the "shiny" she had seen from forty yards away in the dark of night. It was a car. There appeared to be no one in it. "Somebody broke down. Lucky thing they could push the car off the road, so no one comes around that corner and hits it," I said.

Gram heard me but didn't answer. Instead, she went over to the car and shined her flashlight inside. There was movement, then I heard her say, "You can't park here! This is private property! This is my driveway! You'll have to leave!"

I just stood there, feeling slightly embarrassed. The driver was running his hands over his hair, and his passenger sat with her hands over her face, peeking through her fingers at Grandma. I was twelve. I knew by then about boy/ girl things—wasn't interested myself yet, but knew about it.

"Okay, we're leaving. I didn't know this was someone's driveway."

"Well, 'tis! And don't park here again!"

She turned to walk back to the house, and I fell into step beside her. We walked in silence, until I said, "I still don't know how you saw something from so far away."

"This is my place, Janis. I see everything." Behind us, we heard the car start up and drive away.

Another time, we were sitting in our spot under the elm tree having lunch. Gram kept looking down toward the lake, also about forty yards away. I looked in the direction she was looking, but all I could see was shoreline, trees, and water.

"There's someone down there. Do you see them?" she asked me. She was staring hard at a spot beside the path, so I looked there. "Do you see that spot on the left side of the path? Somebody's there."

"I see something, Gram. It looks like a tree stump."

"That ain't no tree stump! Somebody's there. Come on, we're going to walk down there."

She went inside to get a bucket. I knew we were going to get water, while we were at it. I picked up a bucket, too.

We walked slowly down the path, stepped on the board that lay across where a small stream of water flowed, pushed branches gently out of our way as we walked, and finally came near the spot on the path where I had seen what I thought was a stump.

A young man stood up and looked at Gram and me. He had not made a sound, or moved, before that.

"This is private property! What are you doing here?" she demanded to know.

"We're fishing." Down on the dock were two more young men, now looking in our direction at the sound of voices.

"You can't fish here! This is private property! Get your stuff and go. They'll let you fish next door at the resort, but you can't fish here." Gram was firm and the boys on the dock were already gathering up their bait and poles. The stump boy was just standing there with his hands in his pockets, looking from Gram's face to mine but saying nothing more. I studied him. He had dark, wavy hair and a rugged-looking face with a dark shadow on his chin and cheekbones. He shaves, I guessed.

Gram saw him looking at me and noticed that I was looking back. "I said, you can't fish here," she repeated for his benefit, "or anything else either. There are girls at the resort next door. You can quit looking at this one. She's not going with you."

I wished that she would let me speak for myself. I was sixteen, old enough to speak for myself, you'd think. I looked at the boy once more, then turned and followed Gram down the other path toward where we would dip our water.

"If you're here when I come back, I'll get the sheriff after you," she called back to the boys. I didn't expect to see the handsome spy again. I wondered if he had been watching me all day, or if he had been supposed to be the lookout for the boys who were fishing. I never found out.

## WHEN IT'S DARK OUTSIDE

WHEN IT'S DARK OUTSIDE, it's time to go to sleep—unless we have company, or unless we are at a powwow, or unless we are someplace other than home. Generally speaking, though, when it's dark outside, it's time to go to sleep.

I learned that from Grandma, who always made it a practice to turn the oil lamp down low and tuck an envelope or other piece of paper outside the glass bulb, just in case the light might keep us awake. It didn't, but it was a comfort to have the little glow in case we had to get up during the night to use the slop pail. We kept the slop pail just inside the door with a log handy to use as a seat if the need arose. Gram always said to "go out" before going to bed—that way you could usually make it through the night without having to use the slop pail. It wouldn't do to go to the outhouse in the middle of the night, because there were bears outside and maybe other creatures that you wouldn't want to surprise or, more to the point, you wouldn't want them to surprise you.

It was nice to look out the window at night and see the stars and the fireflies. Gram's shack was about a city block from the lake and on nights with a full moon, we could see the reflections on the water. She always made sure the trees and grass were cleared to keep that view of the lake. It isn't like that anymore. It's all grown over, so I guess the only place that view exists nowadays is in my mind.

It was cozy in our little shack. We had mice and snakes close by, always trying to come inside to get warm, but they usually didn't make it. We could hear them sometimes at night, rustling around in the walls. Dad came over and banked all around the house with sand to keep the creatures out. When the weather started to turn cold, I felt sorry for them, because here I was in a warm, soft bed, and there they were scurrying around trying to find a place to get warm, too.

Gram kept a low fire going in our wood burner through the night. When I was a girl, up to about age twelve, I slept with Gram on her feather tick mattress. It was fun watching her get ready for bed. She had a nice routine of getting me ready and in bed first. I waited and watched while she washed up, rolled an oatmeal paste on her face, washed it off, applied a layer of Noxema, and combed her long hair before coiling it up again in a horizontal ringlet at the nape of her neck. She favored flannel nightgowns, and so did I. She smelled wonderful and felt all warm and soft when she finally came to bed.

And she had the book. The book was any book she happened to be reading to me on a given night. She would read only one chapter at a time, so I went to sleep wondering what would happen next to the characters who were being revealed to me night after night. It was a wonderful way to go to sleep.

After she read to me, she usually read a bit from her little bible, too, but not aloud. She had taught me one prayer to say before going to sleep, and the rest of any religious instruction she left alone. She had other spiritual influences that were not really stated either but became apparent to me by observation, and soon I knew of other beliefs that were important also.

Sometimes Gram would be so silly. Like when she knew I wasn't sleeping yet, so to get me to relax and go to sleep she would make noises like she was in deep slumber. I would be looking at her eyes, trying to see a glimmer of something, anything shiny, to give her away, but she was good at keeping her eyelids together and still knowing that I was watching her. She started to say "poooooo," then she would take a little breath in and wait a couple of seconds, then say "poooooo" again.

I let her say "poooooo" about five times before I giggled. Then she said, "Go to sleep, now. That's enough!"

I gave her a little kiss on the cheek and took one more sniff of her Noxema, then rolled over and went to sleep.

## RAISIN BREAD BIRTHDAY PARTY

WE WERE POOR, as in we had no extra money. I didn't expect a cake for my birthday, especially since my birthday fell right between Christmas and New Year's. Everyone was just calming down from the Christmas festivities and getting ready for the New Year's ball to drop. It was time to put away the red and green and begin making resolutions for the coming year, about how to become a better person and all that. It was not time to think about someone who had the nerve to be born in the middle of all of this annual hassle.

As usual, during the holiday break from school, I was out in the country with Gram. This particular year I'm remembering, one of my sisters and my cousin were there, too. On my birthday, I woke up feeling a little different. Older. Old. I mean, this year I would be ten. That meant two digits in my age instead of only one. I had to get a tablet and write it down: 10. That looked like a substantial change. I wrote 9 next to it, just to see the change in black and white. 9, 9, 9, 9, 9 . . . now 10, 10, 10, 10, 10. I wanted to get dressed and go outside so I could write it in the snow. I wanted to walk down to the lake and sit on my rock and think about what the new year would mean to me, being ten and all. Would I still be skinny? Would my freckles start to go away? Would I still get all As in school, or was it time for me to start looking at boys? If I did start to look at boys, would they look back? Would I want them to?

It was just too much to think about. I rolled over and hugged Gram's pillow. She was already up, had a fire going, and was cooking breakfast. Just like any other day. I knew it was oatmeal this morning, but I could smell cinnamon, too, and toast. We put canned milk and sugar on our oatmeal sometimes, and sometimes we put bacon pieces and salt and pepper. This morning, I could tell it would be milk and sugar.

"Come on, girls, it's almost ready. Patsy, you and Rose Emma get washed up first, then come and help me. Janis, you beat that feather tick with a broom first before you make the bed, then get washed up."

Oh, sure, it's *my* birthday, but they get to wash up first! And I have to make the bed! I thought grumpily, even though I liked making the bed, beating the feather tick with a broom and watching it get nice and fluffy.

I let my mind wander as I beat the feathers fluffy. I went to a birthday party once when I was about eight years old. It was a block up the hill from where we lived in the city. The people who gave their daughter the party had a house that covered the whole block. It wasn't a block, really, just the triangular piece of land where a three-way intersection met. But to me it seemed like a huge park. There was enough room on the lawn to have a picnic! Which is exactly what I did once. Awful little kid, I guess.

All I knew was that there was this big piece of green lawn with beautiful yellow flowers growing all over it. The yard that we had in front of our house in the city was all gravel and rocks. It wasn't our house; we rented the downstairs and other people rented the upstairs. Before we rented it, we had lived in the country, and I remembered lots of trees, grass, and flowers all over the place. Oh, how I missed that.

Anyway, this neighbor's yard was a good place for a picnic, so I brought a little blanket, a glass jar filled with Kool-Aid, and chocolate chips that Mom had in the pantry. I lay down on the blanket and soaked up the warmth from the sun as I watched the few clouds drifting very slowly against the clear blue sky. I put my hands behind my head to form a pillow and drew my knees up into an arched position. I was comfortable, warm, and sniffing every once in a while to get a whiff of the grass and earth. They smelled so good!

Something moved and caught my attention. The curtains in the house were pulled to one side and a woman was looking out. Then, at her side, only lower, another face. The girl who lived there was looking at me, then saying something to the lady who, I guessed, must be her mother. I wondered if they were going to come out and send me away. I sat up and leaned on my hand while I waited for the worst. But nothing happened. I was about to lie down again when I saw someone running at me from across the street.

Oh, no, it's that kid with the blond hair who always looks so dirty. Dirty face, dirty hands, dirty clothes, dirty fingernails. Yuck!

Yep, here he comes, and he had a bow and arrow in his hands. "What is this, a stickup?" I asked him.

"Just hand over the goodies and you won't get hurt," he said. I looked up at him as he held the bow with one hand and pulled back the string with the other, aiming the arrow with its rubber tip at my face.

"Cut it out now. These are the only chocolate chips I have. Go home and get your own!"

"Nope, these aren't yours anymore. They're mine now. Get off the blanket!"

I got off the blanket and threw my handful of chocolate

chips at him. He reached down and grabbed the bag, after transferring his arrow to his left hand along with the bow. "You creep! I'm the Indian here, not you!" I looked disdainfully at his piddly little bow and arrow. "Besides, you're a boy, and I'm a girl. You're not very brave at all if you have to steal candy from girls."

He was backing away from me with the bag of candy held fast in his hand. He pointed a finger at me. "Don't try to follow me. It won't do you any good!"

"I wouldn't follow you, and I don't even want the candy now. Not after you touched it! Ick!"

That was the best I could do with insults as I watched him take off with my picnic goodies. I looked back at the window in the house, but there was no movement. Why weren't they looking out when it would have done me good? They could have stopped the robber.

I was thinking about all of this as I whacked the feather tick hard with the broom. A feather floated out and up in the air. Ooops! Too hard. I better quit.

As I put the sheets and blankets in place, I thought again about the birthday party I went to. I wasn't invited; I was just visiting the big green lawn again one day. All of a sudden, kids started coming. They were in party clothes, carrying pretty wrapped packages with ribbons on them. I watched as the door opened and each kid went in. After a while, the little girl who lived there came out and asked me to come in. I said, "I can't, I don't have a present. I wasn't invited." Her mom appeared beside her and smiled at me. "You don't need a present. And we just invited you." I went in, thinking all white people aren't mean after all. Boy, was it a good party. We all got to wear little peaked hats and eat candy, and we all got prizes for playing games. Prizes for playing games?

I could hardly believe it. Playing the game was fun enough, but the winner got to pick out a prize, too.

Everyone there got a prize of some kind. I got a prize for dropping the most clothespins in a glass milk bottle. I was good at it because I often played with clothespins.

There, the bed is made. I'm all washed up and ready for breakfast. And today I'm ten!

Gram sat at the head of the table, I sat on her right-hand side, Rose Emma sat on her left-hand side, and Patsy sat at the other end of the table. Before we ate, Gram always said grace. After grace, she told me to look under my saucer. Money! One shiny dime and two bright pennies. "Happy Birthday," they all said at once.

"Thank you," I said, smiling as hard as I could. "And I got money! Thank you. Dimes are better than pennies, though," I announced.

"Shame on you!!" Gram said, her face stern. Gram was hardly ever stern, so I wondered what I had done to bring shame on myself.

"Do you want the girls to take their pennies back?" she asked me. I looked at my cousin and my sister, and they were looking at me, not smiling. I felt my face heat up. I hadn't thought where the pennies had come from, or the dime for that matter. I was just sizing up the value in terms of what it could buy, not in terms of what it had cost the people who had given them to me.

"I'm sorry," I whispered, feeling myself getting ready to cry. "I like the pennies, too. I didn't mean that they weren't any good." My cousin reached over and patted my hand, and my sister came around to hug me. "Happy Birthday, Jan," she said. Then she gave me a little kiss on the cheek.

We're not rich. I didn't expect a cake, or a party or fancy

wrapped presents. And as Gram told me later, "Just be grateful for what you have. And remember to say thank you. Nobody has to give you anything, and if they do, you remember where it came from."

At breakfast, after I had my little lesson in gratitude, Gram went to the kitchen and brought back a saucer that had toasted slices of raisin bread on it. "It's your birthday, and we couldn't have cake, but we've got raisin bread, and that's just as good as cake."

It is, too. I have it every year on my birthday, as I remember how the tradition started and all of the other lessons in life I learned from my grandmother.

This year I'll be seventy-nine, so the memory of my winter birthday celebration of sixty-nine years ago is well ingrained in me, as are all the other little lessons I've learned along the way.

"Just be grateful for what you have . . . nobody has to give you anything." Oh, the power of those words. This year, I feel grateful for so many things. In our big family, I had six sisters and brothers. Although the three brothers are gone, we sisters are still here to remember our brothers, to share memories, and, every once in a while, to make new ones. I feel grateful that we had a good mother who taught us things along the way, too. Unlike Grandma, Mom rarely said things in so many words. She just did them, and the lessons caught up with us later.

In 2001, our first Christmas without Mom here, I had a chance to think about things a little more than usual. I heard the usual Christmas carols and seasonal music on the radio, and one song, the old Elvis version of "Blue Christmas," caught my attention. "I'll have a blue Christmas without you. I'll be so blue just thinking about you. Decorations of red on a green Christmas tree won't be the same, dear, if you're not here with me," and I thought how awful it must be if someone really felt that lonely. Mom lives inside me, along with all the other dear ones who have walked on. That year I put up a small memory tree in honor of Mom. It was three feet tall and stood brightly decorated on the glass table three feet away from the other tree in the living room.

At the base of the memory tree, a sparkly layer of fake snow surrounded the trunk, and two little elves sat watching a skater glide across a smooth sheet of ice to a waltz tune. One elf was wearing a green tunic with a matching green poinsettia-shaped collar, with two round gold buttons tacked fashionably in front, bib style. A pair of green-and-white-striped baggy pants with green cuffs completed the ensemble, along with a green peaked cap with a gold bell at the tip, which hung jauntily forward. The other elf was wearing a one-piece red-and-white-striped pajama-style outfit with red collar and cuffs at the arms and legs. He also wore a peaked cap, red with a single bell at the tip, which pointed straight back, giving the effect that the red elf was moving forward at a fast rate of speed. Both elves were barefoot and wide-eyed, with curly blond hair tumbling out from under their hats. They each had a healthy sprinkling of freckles on their cheeks and sweetly pursed lips, as though they had pleasant secrets to share.

Above the elves, long strands of icicles shimmered and shone, especially when anyone walked by. These elves were and are a real treasure to me, as they are identical to two that I gave Mom years back. There are other elves in that family, but I had selected this pair for Mom and me so we would have a matching set. She took the two elves, turned them over and over in her hands, and then looked at me over the rim of her glasses. "Where are the rest of them?" she asked. "I know there are more." I started laughing, wishing I had gotten us the complete set, but looking again at the two I had chosen, I told her, "These elves are special," and we let it go at that. I recall seeing her tiny elves on display along with her doll collection, so she decided they were special, too.

Small ceramic angels graced the branches of the tree, along with one soft furry white angel wearing a gold crown and lacy frock of full blue netting and holding a three-dimensional sparkling white and silver snowflake edged in gold. Her golden wings pointed gracefully toward the star at the top of the tree. Three hundred twinkling mini lights of blue cast magical highlights on the snow beneath the tree and on the glittered snowballs that nestled in the boughs of the branches. Overall, the feeling of my blue Christmas was soft, sparkling, safe, and oh so sweet with memories of Mom.

The other tree was decorated in multicolored lights and stood six feet tall. At the base was the ever-present layer of glittering snow. Hanging from the branches of the green spruce were various trimmings from years past and new ones from that year. Red birds on gold branches against a clear globe of glass, subtle mint-green frosted globes, off-white luminescent snowflake bulbs of assorted sizes, and old-fashioned big multicolored light covers for the tiny mini lights. I think of the beliefs that can be celebrated at Christmas, and of how those beliefs overlap like the decorations used that year. We had a small set of votive light candleholders that were reminiscent of the red and cobalt glass lights in a Catholic church. Our votive lights were red, blue, purple, gold, and green. We had no candles in them. We just let them sit and reflect the lights around them. The multicolors were a good imitation of the northern lights, which are beautiful to witness and have a special meaning to Ojibwe people.

One thing becomes increasingly clear: life is one long lesson in love. You have it, you give it, you treasure it, and you never lose it once you've experienced it. And it comes in different forms. Here and now, yesterday, and far away, tomorrow, and forever, but life's lessons are always there for you.

How lucky I am to have lived so long and under so many good influences.

## THE STRENGTH OF WOMEN

GRANDMA KEPT HER LONG HAIR CLEAN and coiled up in a long, thick, horizontal ringlet at the nape of her neck. She favored the oversize V-shaped hairpins to keep it in place. Each night before going to bed, she took the pins out and brushed her hair, carefully removing the loose strands and making little loose hairballs out of them to store them away in a secret place. I used to wonder why she saved the hair. One night I finally asked her about it.

She told me that hair is the strength of women and women are the strength of the people. Hmmm. Simple enough.

I wanted to know more.

Part of who you are and where you came from is in your hair. You won't know the answer to a question sometimes. But the people who lived before you might have known the answer. Get that hair and hang on to it, then think about your question. You might get an answer. Your ancestors knew things that people don't know anymore.

I thought about the things she told me, and her stories made sense. Hair grows on a baby even before it's born, and it grows on people even after they walk on. There is strength in hair.

I used to do an experiment to see how strong my hair was. I would take a strand and challenge people to use a strand of their hair to see if it would cut mine. The process was simple. I would hold my strand of hair taut between my left and right hand and the other person would hold their strand the same way. Then we would put the two strands together and push them at a crosswise angle against one another until one of the strands broke. Mine never broke. So I had to believe it when Gram said hair is a woman's strength and that hair had special powers. Do I save the hair from my hairbrush? Sometimes I do and sometimes I let it fly in the wind so the birds can use it to line their nests. I want them to have strong nests, so we can enjoy the beauty of their songs and so their babies will be warm.

What do I do with the hair I save? I use it as I was instructed. When I have a serious question where the answer eludes me, I hold the hair bundle in my hand and talk to the ancestors, asking for advice and guidance. They always watch over us and are ready to answer our petitions, especially when we ask our questions in old, familiar ways.

When Grandma grew old and went to a nursing home for a while until Mom traveled to Minnesota to get her, the people there cut her hair short. They said it was easier to take care of. And although by then Grandma's hair had grown silver and thinner, I could see the sadness in her eyes when I visited her, and she said, "Here I am, with my old bald head."

I took out my hairbrush and gently brushed her hair,

cleaning the brush as I worked. "Don't worry, Gram. Your hair will grow back," was the only thing I could think to say. I had brought her a package of gray V-shaped hairpins, the kind she liked, and I put them inside her bedside table. I placed her hair from the hairbrush into a tissue and plucked one of my own hairs to tie the tissue with. "There, now," I said. She watched me make the hair bundle and then she smiled. "Oh, Janis, you always show your love for me," she said.

With a woman like Gram, it was easy to show love. She told me stories and got me to think about things in new ways. I can see ages and ages of strands of hair linking generations together and binding past generations to future generations in a never-ending cycle. From the women come the children and from the children come the people who will make more children. So, as we become ancestors, our children will look to us for advice and guidance, if we give them the tools to communicate now. Grandma gave me tools to communicate, and I feel safe.

## GOD HELPS THOSE WHO HELP THEMSELVES

EARLY IN THE MORNING, Grandma got up and put wood in the stove to cook and to heat the irons for ironing our clothes. Sunday was a special day, and it meant wearing special clothes and taking a long walk to church. Sometimes we got a ride, sometimes we didn't. It depended on who was driving down the road at the time. As long as the weather was warm, we walked. Gram didn't own a car. She never wanted one. We always got to where we needed to go.

After the fire was going good in the stove, Gram heated

water for me to wash with and started cooking breakfast
while I washed my face and got dressed for my walk to the
mailbox. The mailbox was a good city block away, so it was
a good wake-up walk. The grass was nice and dewy, and
sometimes there were puddles to admire from a recent
rainfall or a spring thaw, depending on the time of the year.
I liked my walks.

I liked getting back to our little palace, too, where Gram
had breakfast ready. After we ate our oatmeal and toast,
or rice with raisins and milk, Gram started the ironing
ritual. She had selected her dress and carefully sprinkled
and ironed it while I looked through a big box of hats and
handkerchiefs for something to wear on my head. In those
days, all the girls and ladies wore something on their heads.
That was in the 1950s, before the Roman Catholic church
made so many changes. Mass used to be in Latin, and I liked
it that way—not that I could understand Latin, but it left me
time to think about things in my own way.

My head covering was usually a scarf folded into a trian-
gle and tied just below my chin. It made me feel very holy,
very nunlike. Grandma was quite religious, having gone to a
boarding school run by German nuns. She had things to say
about the experience, but I won't repeat that part. And I'll
also add that I get the feeling that she was quite a spiritual
person even before that. She had a way of letting you know
that you ought to be thankful for what you have and not be
wishing for more. I know she worked hard for what she had,
and it seemed like a great deal.

Well, I took a long time trying on hats and scarves just
for the fun of it. To this day, I love to wear hats and have fun
trying them on. I still love oatmeal and Latin masses, too.

By the time we were ready to go, the sun had been up

for at least an hour. We put the padlock on the door and set out on our two-mile hike to the little log church next to the graveyard. We usually stopped in the graveyard before or after church because that's where my Uncle Ralph, Grandma's son who was killed in World War II, is buried. She told me once that someone asked her how she knew it was him, since they sent him home in a closed casket. She said she just knew.

The church we went to was located next to the Indian cemetery in Sawyer, Minnesota, on the Fond du Lac Indian reservation. White folks went to that church, too. In fact, mostly white folks went there. We had white neighbors in the cottages around the lake. The Indians lived in wooden houses along dirt roads near the church. After church, we would visit them sometimes.

There was a wooden structure in front of the church that had a picture painted on the back wall of Lily of the Mohawks. She was of the Mohawk tribe and on her way to sainthood, even then. Gram took me to see the painting more than once but never said much about it.

The church was built of logs and was old. It was only one room with an altar at the front and two rows of pews, one on either side of the center aisle. It was small, and usually all of the pews were filled. There were stained glass windows that were quite beautiful. I never thought much about the sermons, just liked to take in all the sights and smells of the place. All of the people wore a certain style of Sunday dress that was pretty predictable. The men wore suits and hats, and there were little latch-type hooks on the backs of the pews for them to hang their hats. The women wore dresses and hats, or scarves, on their heads and kept them on for the whole mass.

In the fifties, women also wore gloves and carried a rosary and a little prayer book. There were also extra prayer books in the pews. I looked at one of the extra ones, as I did not have one of my own. Gram did, though she did not usually bring it to church. She used one of theirs also. Her rosary was plain black wooden beads. Other women had colored crystal rosaries, and those were the ones I liked to look at. It was just so churchy to see so many colored crystals glistening in the sunlight that came through the stained glass windows! It felt good to see so many people being good and looking kind and smelling like talcum powder. There was incense in the church that smelled good, too. But by the time mass was over, I was glad to be able to go outside and smell the evergreen trees that grew outside the church.

Sometimes we went to bake sales that were held right out under those huge evergreen trees. The ladies set their cakes and pies and cupcakes and cookies on plates covered with clear wrap on tables that had been set up under the trees. If we bought anything, it was usually an apple pie. Then we had to hope for a ride home, so we wouldn't have to carry that pie for two miles.

There were days when the priest would ring the bell that sat in a belfry just above the front door. As small as the church was, it still had two doors. Sometimes we would go out the back door and follow the path into the woods behind the church, just to go for a walk. There was much to be seen in those woods: trees, flowers, ferns, birds, berry bushes. The sounds and colors could be heard and seen keenly, because we were out in the country. It was a blessing and wonderful gift from the Creator that there were no city sounds to drown out the sounds of nature.

Walking in the woods was a common pastime for Gram and me. We talked about things on our walks to and from church and other places. The walks provided stories to remember and tell, but one at a time. "Watch out for the gift of gab. . . . Children should be seen and not heard. . . . There's a time and place for everything." These were Grandma's sayings that she inserted every once in a while into our conversations, especially if I started asking too many questions when she was trying to tell me something. And I was always asking questions.

One time I was asking her about going to the Indian boarding schools, and I was asking questions more than once. I knew I was doing that, but I wanted to make sure I got all the details right. She repeated her answers a couple of times, then I would ask the same question a separate way. Finally, she said, "Well, Janis, I guess you're kinda dumb!"

I laughed and said, "Yes, Gram, I *am* kinda dumb! I don't know anything, and I'm trying to understand these things!" "These things" were details of her experience in the boarding schools, her feelings about being punished for speaking Ojibwe, and about being so far away from home when she was in school. We talked about all of that more than once. She said it wasn't easy being there and that she missed her mother, but she took this opportunity to tell me that God never gives you more hardship than you can bear. You have to be willing to work for what you get and be willing to bear your own burdens with dignity. She liked to point out the Stations of the Cross to me and tell me how Jesus carried his cross and we all have our crosses to bear. Nobody else can do it for you.

"Always remember, Janis, that God helps those who help themselves."

Well, you can see how our walks gave me valuable information about Grandma's experiences and beliefs and gave me things to think about. I'm still thinking about them.

After church, if we decided to go visiting and the adults started talking Chippewa, well, we kids just knew that we might as well get lost, because they didn't want us to know what they were saying. And they didn't want us to know it so badly that they were talking the forbidden language to keep their secrets. So, okay. It was more fun to go and play in the dirt anyway, or in the fern patches we always managed to find. This was the country, mind you. That's why I said sometimes we walked and sometimes we rode. It depended on which neighbor wanted to go to church that day.

I mean, we didn't get into cars with just anyone who came along. Grandma was really careful about that. She told me about one time that she did get into a car with a stranger, a man who picked her up on the road to Cloquet. She worked in Cloquet as a housecleaner, and she was so good at it. She took me to cleaning jobs with her sometimes and showed me how to clean things right, so now I'm good at it, too—keeping a clean house, I mean. Well, anyway, the time the strange man picked her up, I was not with her. She was alone with him in the car and trying to have a pleasant conversation like she always did with our drivers. But this guy had something else on his mind. And he pulled it out and let it lie in his lap. So Gram just kept on talking about the weather, the scenery, and the road and a thousand other neutral topics, never letting on that she had seen his main topic at all. Finally, he just put it away and at the end of the ride, he apologized to her for what he had done. He said he didn't know what got into him. Gram said, "Some guys are like that, so you got to be careful."

She used to favor reading true detective stories so she would know what was going on in the world, and what she learned was that "you can't be too careful." I read a couple of the stories, but they were not as thrilling to me as stories like *Black Beauty* and *Cinderella,* two of my favorite bedtime stories from Grandma that I heard at about age eight. *Black Beauty* and *Cinderella* thrilled me with their characterizations of a horse, mice, and birds that could think and feel like humans do. I've always thought that all creatures must be able to think and feel, and I'm careful to treat them with respect and kindness, the way I want to be treated. When I got a little older, I favored biographies. They told me about what was going on in the world and gave me insight into how people thought and why they acted the way they did. But I can think of nothing that gave me more insight into life than spending those leisurely Sundays with Grandma, walking to the old log cabin church and hearing her stories.

GRAM'S BEEN GONE for forty-four years now, since March 18, 1981, but not really. She's right here in my heart and sometimes in my head.

I'm thinking that if God helps those who help themselves, then the help I got in coping with Grandma's funeral came from the God we visited so many times in the old log church. I remember the pain of loss after the funeral, when I thought I could help myself by visiting the old log church again.

Her funeral mass was held in the new brick church that was on the same property. The new church didn't have the same feel or smell or memories that the old church had. Gram went to mass for years in the new church, after they closed the log cabin church, but I never went to church there with her. It wasn't a great comfort to me to see her casket in the front of that altar in the brick building.

Somehow I ended up in the front row right next to Gram's casket. Mom was next to me, and I kept a close eye on her, feeling very keenly that she must be going through her own turmoil over losing her mother. My uncle, Mom's brother, was in the pew directly behind us with his family. They were the last two of Gram's children who were still alive.

As we proceeded out of the church after the funeral, the priest directed me to follow the casket, which I did until we reached the door to go outside. I turned, and now my uncle was behind me, with his hat covering his face as he walked. Behind him was my mother. I stepped back and let my uncle and my mother pass me, then joined the line again after Mom went by. It was only right that her children walk those last few steps to the waiting hearse with her. I was there close to her at the end, as I had always been when she was alive.

After we finished all of the formalities for Gram at the brick church, I went, by myself this time, over to the log cabin church to sit and recall our trips inside. I came to the front door of the church with its single door opening and found that familiar small porch with wooden railings and only one step. I sat down on the step. The sight and feel of the old gray wood provided a certain measure of comfort. The doors had wooden boards nailed across them, but someone had torn off one of the boards. After a couple of minutes, I got up and walked around to the side of the structure. I could see that the back door hung open. I looked inside and saw that there was still a statue intact on the altar. It looked like vandals weren't interested in destroying statues, just in finding a place to get warm.

Two jingle dress dancers: my beloved grandmother *(facing page)* around 1934, my teacher, my mentor, wearing her regalia, and me in 1985, the granddaughter of a great matriarch who is always by my side. I loved and respected my grandmother so much; all my life I have wanted to be just like her. Here we are, both at age thirty-nine, two generations apart, but my desire to be like Grandma is evident in the pose I chose for my picture. These pictures hang side by side in my home office.

Wandering slowly, I visited the Lily of the Mohawks shrine, and the painting of the near saint could still be seen. There was no glass in the structure anymore, and people had dropped trash inside, or the wind had blown it there. The evergreen trees that surrounded the church now dwarfed it and cast long shadows all around. It felt cool in the middle of the day.

I dropped ceremonial tobacco into the open shrine and asked that Lily take loving care of Gram now. I felt sure that she would recognize her right away.

In a distance, I could hear the echoes of the workers trying to lengthen the grave. Gram's casket was too long to fit into the hole they had dug, so they were working to make the hole longer.

I went back to sit on the church step again. I smiled as the digging noises continued. "Just not quite ready to go yet, eh, Gram?"

I was still listening to the diggers' noises when my cousin came walking up the bigger set of stairs that led from the parking lot up the hill to the church.

"Come to the hall. Everybody's looking for you. It's time to eat," she said.

"I was just sitting here thinking about Gram."

"We all are. Come on, now. I'll walk with you," she said with tears in her eyes. I gave her a hug and said I was ready to go anyway. I looked in the direction of the cemetery and thought, "Thanks, Gram. See you later." Then we walked away.

# Epilogue

IT'S FUN TO WATCH the little grandmothers when they dance. They are so small, their little feet are so dainty, and their smiles are so sweet. They come and dance in a circle behind me as I dance, watching and following my footsteps. Sometimes their tiny fingers find their way into one of my jingle cones and I dance a bit slower so their curious hands and eyes can make a proper survey and they don't cut their tiny fingers by the sharp edges of the cones on my dance dress. I recall the first time I understood that the little grandmothers-in-training were following me in the dance circle. I had been dancing at a powwow, deep in prayer as I often am while I dance. Someone took a picture of me as I danced and later gave me a copy. As I looked at the picture, I saw the little girls in line behind me, eyes on my moccasins as I danced. They're learning from me, I thought, as I examined each intent little face. They had not said a word and I had not known that they were dancing behind me, watching my steps.

Suddenly I felt old. My heart filled with love for these children and with the memory of my grandmother, who had led me into the dance circle by the hand and danced with me when I was a little girl. I remember watching her moccasins as she danced and I remember slipping my small fingers inside her jingle cones, as the young children do with me today. I was struck by the realization that I am now a grandmother, and these young children will be grand-mothers one day, with trails of children following behind them. This continuity is as it should be. It is at once a joy and a great responsibility to see that the circle continues.

These days, I see them everywhere, these little grand-mothers-in-training. Always, they come into the circle danc-ing, watching their elders dance, and looking with intent faces at the actions of those who go before them. I embrace them when I see them. I say, "Hello, Little Grandma," and dance beside them when I can. I've seen one girl grow from childhood to young adulthood, who still dances, smiles, embraces me, and returns my greeting at the powwows. "Hello, Little Grandma," I say to her. With a smile, she says, "Hello, Big Grandma," and side by side we dance as a trail of little grandmothers-in-training follows along behind us.

Dancing at the powwow in Sault Ste. Marie, Michigan, in 1992, with two little grandmothers-in-training dancing behind me.

# Acknowledgments

Several people encouraged me in my storytelling as I grew up, but primarily my grandmother, *Nay-ta-baa-ca-co-na-mo-quay*. This is what Grandma (Cecelia Robinson) gave as her Indian name to a reporter while dancing for the students at Washington School in 1973. In the double vowel system of spelling, her name would be *Netaa-baakaakonamookwe*. One translation might be "good opener woman"; another might be "woman who opens doors for someone." Either way, my grandmother, Cecelia Robinson, who sent me on walks through the woods and asked me what I saw on each daily walk, certainly did open doors for me by teaching me how to be aware of my surroundings. I had to tune in, hone all my senses, watch, and describe what trees were doing, what animals were singing and chattering about, what the water was doing and saying, and with each successive walk I had to add more detail. "The wind is gently blowing today" may be true, but by the third windy day I learned to say things like "when the wind blows through the trees on a day like today, the leaves like to whisper secrets, and I like to listen." Grandma liked to tell me stories, too, so we traded tales and techniques often, not in so many words but just by listening to each other. To her I am eternally grateful.

I had a large nuclear family growing up, and I thank my parents, William John Fairbanks Jr. and Alvina Fairbanks Caldwell, and my six siblings for our brief time together and for our interactions that are memorable to me. My sisters, Arleen, Patricia, and Phyllis, and my brothers, Ralph, Gary (Joe), and Gerald (Jerry), all contributed to my stories and memories by allowing me the chance to experience all the feelings and emotions that arise while growing up in a big family. Later additions to our blended family, Bernard Caldwell and Janet Caldwell, have their places in my memories and stories. Family influences certainly are powerful and lasting.

My gratitude extends to my husband, Kazimierz Roterman, my rock, and our son, John Roterman. Both have been my sounding boards and supporters in all that I do.

My circle of literary friends has given me positive feedback when I have helped edit their work or done readings for them. The late Peter Razor, author of *While the Locust Slept*, entrusted me with three of his manuscripts to edit. Another friend, prolific and popular author Marcie Rendon, went a step further, encouraging me to submit my manuscript after she heard me read one of my stories. Without her push in the right direction, this book would not have become a reality. She recommended that I send my manuscript to Erik Anderson, senior editor at the University of Minnesota Press. To Erik Anderson, editorial assistant Emma Saks, and copy editor Louisa Castner, I extend my heartfelt thanks for their editorial skills and for leading me through the editorial process. If any mistakes slipped through into the book, they belong to me. Mistakes are like that spirit bead that invariably appears when you least expect it, and that's okay.

Finally, in the spirit world, I send special thoughts to all my relatives, and especially to Margaret Robinson, my auntie who welcomed my visits and called me to check on me when she hadn't heard from me in a while. She was generous in sharing family history, and now she walks among the stars.

*Miigwech,* thank you.

**JANIS A. FAIRBANKS** is a member of the Fond du Lac Band of Lake Superior Chippewa. Her interests and research are in Native American history and culture, literature, and the Ojibwe language. She works to preserve and revitalize the Ojibwe language and was the first coordinator of the Anishinaabemowin Ojibwe Language Program for the Fond du Lac Reservation.